ADVANCE PRAISE FOR BALANCING ACT

Kitt describes her struggle to manage bipolar disorder in *Balancing Act*. Her profound knowledge of herself enhances her coping abilities as she learns to avoid triggers that will likely exacerbate her symptoms. She reminds readers that medication can only go so far and that a wide array of tools are needed to keep the illness under control. This book will bring comfort, validation, hope, and education, especially to anyone with bipolar disorder.

Lynn Nanos, LICSW, author of *Breakdown: A Clinician's Experience in a Broken System of Emergency Psychiatry*, LynnNanos.com

***

Balancing Act: Writing Through a Bipolar Life is an extraordinarily useful, fascinating book. Kitt O'Malley shares rich insights about living with bipolar disorder as she navigates being a mother, a caregiver for her aging parents, and much more. *Balancing Act* is imbued with compelling honesty. Written from a place of compassion informed by Kitt's background as a psychotherapist, this account will help anyone affected by bipolar disorder. *Balancing Act* is a refreshing and original addition to mental health literature!

Dyane Harwood, Author, *Birth of a New Brain—Healing from Postpartum Bipolar Disorder*, DyaneHarwood.wordpress.com

***

Kitt O'Malley offers us her raw personal journey into a life with bipolar disorder. Her writing style gives the reader an intimate sense of how bipolar mood swings can both energize and fragment a devoted wife, mother, daughter, writer, volunteer, and professional therapist. But, *Balancing Act* also reminds us of the importance of self-care in managing a mental illness. Her struggle to define personal boundaries reflects the painful dilemma that caretakers often experience, especially when they're suffering in silence. Kitt's resolve to accept her personal limits brought by bipolar disorder permits others to care compassionately for themselves.

Michael G. Pipich, MS, LMFT, psychotherapist, and author of *Owning Bipolar: How Patients and Families Can Take Control of Bipolar Disorder*, MichaelPipich.com

***

In *Balancing Act,* the brilliant, accomplished blogger, author, and mental health advocate, Kitt O'Malley, provides a finite road map and a brutally honest glimpse inside the daily frustrations of living with mental illness. Sharing her 20-year struggle with jarring and frank openness, O'Malley's time as a psychotherapist provides a fresh approach and ability to dissect mental illness while sharing a window inside her fears, frustrations, the quest for balance and med stability. O'Malley's honesty is both unique and refreshing. Her unconventional willingness to share her hard-earned nuggets of wisdom and knowledge is a precious gift to survivors and mental health advocates.

Balancing Act is a treasure trove of experience, tender and raw poetry, and a deep dive inside mental illness. Insurmountable faith and love of family are the threads that keep O'Malley grounded and alive. As a writer, I was inspired. As a survivor of Bipolar Disorder, I was enthralled. As a mental health advocate, I was humbled and grateful. *Balancing Act* is an absolutely vital resource, and Kitt O'Malley is the unconventional, necessary mental health ally, doting wife and mother, balancing life with mental illness.

Jacqueline Cioffa, author of *The Red Bench: A Descent and Ascent into Madness,* and novels *The Vast Landscape* and *Georgia Pine*, JacquelineCioffa.com

***

Kitt O'Malley is an awesome advocate and an excellent storyteller. Her honesty shines through on each page of her book and gives the reader a glimpse into life with bipolar disorder.

Gabe Howard, author of *Mental Illness is an Asshole and Other Observations*, host of *The Psych Central Podcast* and co-host of *A Bipolar, A Schizophrenic, And A Podcast*, mental health speaker, GabeHoward.com

Balancing Act

Writing Through a Bipolar Life

Kitt O'Malley

Cover and Interior Design:
Michelle Hammer of Hammer Time Design

DEDICATION

Dedicated to my beloved and devoted husband Nick, who has stood by my side for more than two decades; to my brilliant, sensitive son Matthew, who has taught me compassion and patience; to my sister, who has kept me grounded throughout life; and to my parents, for rescuing me when I could not care for myself, and for teaching me to think critically and develop my intellect.

AKNOWLEDGEMENTS

My husband is my biggest supporter and caretaker. Nick, I couldn't have done any of this without you by my side.

Thanks to Sarah Fader for believing in my work enough to publish it. Aaron J. Smith's excellent and honest book coaching and editing have shaped this work into its final form. I thank Wendy Garfinkle and Katherine Walsh for their expert final editing and proofreading. Michelle Hammer rocked the cover design and interior formatting.

Thank you to my foreword authors, David Susman, PhD, and Steve Pitman, whose steadfast support means the world to me. I'm blown away by the advance praise for *Balancing Act* offered by Lynn Nanos, LICSW, Dyane Harwood, Michael Pipich, LMFT, Jacqueline Cioffa, and Gabe Howard. Shout out to my Balancing Act Street Team and my advance copy readers for their support in helping me build momentum as the publication date neared.

Dyane Harwood, author of *Birth of a New Brain: Healing from Postpartum Bipolar Disorder*, I thank for her friendship, and for including my site in her book's appendix of Blogs by Moms with Postpartum Bipolar Disorder.

There are far too many people for me to thank everyone. I'm a part of a wonderful mutually supportive community of mental health advocates and writers. NAMI Orange County (namioc.org) and OC Writers (ocwriters.network), in particular, empowered me to find and use my voice.

Thank you for reading,

Kitt O'Malley

CONTENTS

XVIII

FOREWORD

By David Susman, PhD

There is a troubling dichotomy in today's system of mental health care.

On the plus side, record numbers now have health insurance, and there is a wide range of effective treatments for mental health conditions, including medications, psychotherapies, and coping skills. Also, more and more people are coming forward and speaking openly about their personal mental health challenges.

Despite these advances, millions of people receive inadequate, ineffective, or no mental health treatment, and the number of suicides increases each year. Many people with severe mental illnesses languish in jails or lie homeless on our streets.

How do we begin to explain this disconnect?

Barriers to mental health care encompass many factors. Some cannot afford to pay for treatment. Many experience shame, anxiety, and fear of being labeled as "mentally ill" or they mistakenly believe that help is not available or that it simply won't work. Friends, family, and society convey uninformed and hurtful messages that mental illnesses are "all in your head" or that you should just "get over" them.

Enter Kitt O'Malley.

Kitt has been one of the leading mental health advocates for several years through her widely-known social media presence and her ground-breaking blog, which has chronicled her lifelong journey with bipolar disorder. Her goals are to affect change, break down barriers to care and to educate people about mental illness. Kitt's perspective is additionally unique in that she is trained as a psychotherapist, and she practiced for a time as a licensed mental health professional.

What you are about to read is a compilation of Kitt's writing, blog posts, and poetry from the past several years. Through her words, you will better understand what it is like to live with bipolar disorder. You will see that Kitt's courage and candor are remarkable. Along the way, you will also learn of the challenges Kitt has faced as a parent and as a caregiver of her own parents.

Kitt's message is a critically important one. She helps us learn that everyone's mental health journey is unique and filled with ups and downs, not unlike the highs and lows of her bipolar disorder. Although Kitt has faced many obstacles, she also brings a clear message of hope. She shows us that mental health treatments can be effective and that a person is not defined by their illness.

Finally, Kitt teaches us that the journey of recovery is an ongoing one and that people who live with a mental illness can not only learn to manage it, but they can ultimately thrive and flourish.

David Susman, PhD
Licensed Psychologist and Assistant Professor
University of Kentucky Department of Psychology
DavidSusman.com

FOREWORD

By Steve Pitman

I've known Kitt O'Malley for years through my work at NAMI. Kitt and I have attended meetings together, shared meals, and engaged in compelling conversation. Kitt is a thoughtful listener, and equally as strong at voicing her opinion. I knew her as a licensed therapist. I only learned that she lived with bipolar disorder when she shared it. Kitt is thoughtful, competent, and professional.

Balancing Act pulls the curtain back on the challenges Kitt confronted and her efforts to overcome them. Notwithstanding those challenges, she leads a happy, healthy life. It's a story of persistence and courage. The book gives readers insight into the way the mind works during mania as well as depression.

Kitt O'Malley looks just like the rest of us. I had no idea the extent of her journey with mental illness until reading her book. Learning her struggles with her mental health, caring for her son, her husband, and her parents, all while dealing with Bipolar disorder, magnifies the respect I have for her. Kitt, in allowing us to look inside your life, you provide a glimmer of what so many people living with mental illness manage. My respect for Kitt's life journey is profound.

Steve Pitman

NAMI Orange County, Orange County, CA

Affiliate President, Board of Directors: 2011 - 2015, 2018 - present   president

NAMI (National Alliance on Mental Illness), Arlington, VA

Member, National Board of Directors, 2015 - 2021

President 2016-2018

PREFACE

Why I Wrote This Book

Welcome to the book publication of my writing from KittOMalley.com. The book starts with an overview of my life with bipolar disorder. Blog posts follow, organized into these major themes: Bipolar Thoughts, Write with Purpose, Advocate, and Caretake. For information about bipolar disorder and mental health resources, see the Appendices.

I wrote this book for those living with bipolar disorder or another mental health diagnosis, those loving someone with mental health issues, and those who want to gain understanding about bipolar disorder.

In sharing my story with you, I aim to educate and inspire. I give hope to those living with bipolar and other mental health diagnoses. I provide insight to those who do not know what it's like to live with this diagnosis.

My social skills enable me to hide my invisible brain disorder from the outside world, from all but those closest to me. This book gives you specific insight into what my bipolar life looks like. You may see me at my best, or what you think of as my best, but do not know what I must cope with, what goes on in my mind.

My story matters to me because I've worked hard to overcome internalized stigma. I've worked hard to accept myself as I am. Living with mental illness is not easy. But, getting professional help, both psychiatric and psychotherapeutic, has made my life easier and has led me to this purposefully written book, and to the work I do as a mental health advocate online, and through my writing.

What follows is a collection of my thoughts, my inner dialogue, which gives the reader insight into my mind, my bipolar thought process, into how I live with bipolar disorder. This book grew out of my blog writing at k to-malley.com, but here I share my writing beyond blog readers.

This book promotes better understanding and compassion for those living with mental illness and for those who love and care for them. I hope to encourage those struggling with mental health issues to get help and to realize that their lives can improve with proper treatment.

Whether or not you live with a mental health diagnosis, your life has purpose. Everyone's life has purpose. We all deserve love, respect, compassion, and kindness.

My Mental Health Journey

As a Child

When my parents introduced me as a child, they always said, "Kitt is going to go to Harvard Medical School and become a doctor when she grows up." By the time I was in high school, I had aspired to become a neurosurgeon. I got almost straight A's, allowing myself a B in physics, was a medical explorer scout, trained as an emergency medical technician, wrote for the school paper, and logged many hours in drama and dance. As a senior, I applied to the schools with the highest acceptance rates into medical school.

Despite my hard-earned achievements, I didn't get into any of those schools. Receiving rejection letter after rejection letter hit me hard. As I grew up, my parents told me that I could go to school anywhere I wanted and could do anything I wanted. Wrong. Instead of attending an East Coast Ivy League school, I started my freshman year at UCLA as a biochemistry major. As the summer after high school graduation approached, I got a letter from UCLA saying I had to take remedial summer courses since my SAT scores totaled under 700. Back in the 1980s the math portion totaled 800, the verbal portion 800. My math score alone was 720 (yes, I was once a math geek). Apparently, the Educational Testing Service incorrectly reported my scores to UCLA. When I showed UCLA my scores, not only did I not have to do remedial work, but I was eligible for College Honors, in which I became active as a freshman.

***

As a College Student

As a freshman at UCLA I fell into a deep depression, believing that my parents, my sister, the whole world would be better off without me alive. When I told my friends of my suicidal thoughts, they made me promise to get professional help. I saw a UCLA psychologist, whose cognitive therapy, also known as cognitive behavioral therapy or CBT, saved my life by helping me rewrite my suicidal thoughts, and stop my suicidal impulses.

If your symptoms are life-threatening, please immediately call 911 (USA and Canada), go to the emergency room, or contact the National Suicide Prevention Lifeline at 1-800-273-8255 (USA).

Depression involves distorted, negative thoughts and beliefs which are "automatic," or outside of conscious awareness. In CBT, I learned how to identify these automatic thoughts and "restructure" them. Changing my thoughts changed the way I felt and behaved.

My CBT homework was to keep thought records where I separated my thoughts and feelings to determine whether those thoughts were true. If my thoughts were negative inaccurate cognitive distortions, I'd replace them with more realistic ones. Using these worksheets, I literally "rewrote" my negative thoughts. Doing so rewires our brains. The neural circuits in my brain used to short-cut to suicidal ideation. Cognitive techniques en-abled me to identify the suicidal and depressive ideas as irrational, stop them, and rewrite (or reason with) them.

Here are the negative inaccurate cognitive distortions that I worked on in cognitive therapy:

"The world would be a better place without me," which is an example of jumping to conclusions and fortune-telling. I did not have evidence to sup-port that conclusion. At the time, I volunteered at the UCLA Medical Center Emergency Room. When I was in high school, I volunteered at local hospi-tals. Even if I didn't volunteer my time to help others, the world would NOT have been better without me. My friends, family, and acquaintances would have been devastated. Unfortunately, depression lies.

In the same vein, I thought, "My family (or my sister) would be better off without me." I believed that they'd have more resources available for my sister if I wasn't such a drain on the family's finances, time, and energy. My reasoning was emotional, not logical. As a Californian, UCLA in the early 1980s was a deal, especially compared to the Ivy League school I had want-ed to attend. This might also be an example of a should thought. I thought I shouldn't have any needs. That my family shouldn't have to support me. I had to think more logically and get rid of those shoulds and shouldn'ts.

Using black-and-white all-or-nothing thinking, I believed, "This pain is un-bearable. I need it to end." Yes, severe suicidal depression hurts. In fact, it can *feel* like a living hell. But it's not hell. Hell is permanent. The pain of severe major depression was temporary. Not only did I bear that hellish pain, but I overcame it.

Believing "I am unworthy of love," I labeled myself negatively. Labeling in-volves making unhelpful overstatements, like "I'm a loser." Of course I was worthy of love. We all are. Not only was I worthy of it, I was loved dearly. I just didn't see it.

I thought, "I am a failure," which involves labeling, overgeneralization, and personalization. An overgeneralization is when you take a single piece of evidence and then infer that it must always be true. I believed that I was a failure because I didn't live up to expectations of attending an Ivy League university, and because I was depressed. I personalized not getting ac-cepted into an Ivy League school and becoming depressed. I saw myself as responsible, when neither were my fault. I worked hard in high school to get into an excellent college. Likewise, depression was not my fault.

"I am ashamed of being depressed. I must be perfect." I expected perfection of myself and was ashamed of my depression. Expecting perfection from myself involves both black-and-white/all-or-nothing thinking and that I should be perfect. No one is perfect. I was, and still am, imperfectly human. As for the shame, that involves internalized stigma (not specifically a cognitive distortion, but I'd argue it is) and personalization.

"I want to die." This thought is an example of catastrophizing. Wanting a permanent, undoable solution, to a fixable problem. Besides, I didn't want to die. I desperately wanted and needed help, which I sought and received.

I told my cognitive psychologist that I had fantasies of being hit by car and hospitalized. He responded, "You can be hospitalized right now." My wish to be hit by a car is an example of a control fallacy, where I'm a victim of an outside force, a car accident. If I needed or wanted psychiatric hospitalization, the UCLA Neuropsychiatric Hospital was available; instead, I persevered in cognitive therapy.

Cognitive therapy helped me overcome severe suicidal depression and gave me a skill I still use today. Unfortunately, my underlying biological-ly based mental illness remained. Very active on campus, I volunteered in UCLA Medical Center Emergency Room, sat on the Executive Council of College Honors as Vice-Chair of their Social Committee (glorified party planner), and trained as a Peer Health Counselor.

For all but my closest friends, I hid behind a facade of competency and social skills. But I was miserable and felt that the biochemistry curriculum was more of a technical training than the well-rounded interdisciplinary education I craved. The August before my sophomore year, I came down with mononucleosis, and used that as an excuse to quit UCLA. I visited family and friends, worked, and attended community college part-time. Then I transferred to UC Berkeley as a legal studies major, a fabulous interdisciplinary program run out of Boalt Hall.

During my junior year at Berkeley, symptoms of depression returned. My mother was diagnosed with non-Hodgkin's lymphoma. I was devastated to learn of my mother's diagnosis. My mother and I researched lymphoma. At the time, studies indicated a five-year prognosis. She pointed out that the medical research we were reading was out of date by the time it was published, that cancer treatment progressed, and life spans increased. She is still alive thirty-five years later thanks to cutting edge monoclonal antibody therapy.

That same academic year, my maternal grandfather died. My grandfather always held a special place in my heart. He was a kindred spirit as a gifted orator (I've always loved the stage) and storyteller (here I am – a writer, a storyteller). The fall after I quit UCLA, I visited him and my grandmother. When he died, it hit me particularly hard. My mother's family asked me to give his eulogy, which was a huge honor. In speaking at his memorial mass, I was carrying on his spirit.

On my way home from the funeral, as I was driving over the San Francisco Bay Bridge, I fell into a trance state brought on by the flashing reflections of the lane markers, and had an out-of-body experience, or more accurately, an in-the-body experience. I felt a tingling all over my body, an energy pushing out, and a warm cleansing energy replacing it. The fact that I was driving over a bridge at the time disturbed me. To test whether I could safely drive, or whether I should put on my hazards and pull over to the side, I put on my turn signal and changed lanes to the right. At the time it seemed safer to continue off the bridge than stop on the bridge.

When I got home, I described the experience to my roommates as a spiritual orgasm. We were interested in spiritual enlightenment, read Alan Watts and D.T. Suzuki, and wanted to experience enlightenment. After that initial spiritual experience, I willfully entered a series of altered states. I would stare into a candle flame, go into a trance state, and enter an altered state of consciousness. The states I entered fell into two basic categories – the light and the dark. The light I would describe as a loss of self that led to clarity – a cleansing. The dark was addictive, as if a siren called me, and threatened a loss of self that could lead to madness. I identified the two experiences as the call of God and the enticement of the Devil and related it to my reading of *The Screwtape Letters* by C.S. Lewis. The dark disguised itself as the light. It was deceitful and dangerous.

In retrospect, I can understand these mystic experiences as the beginning of a hypomanic episode, or mood cycling. At the time, given my history of depression, I knew if I went to a mental health professional and described the experiences, they would diagnose me with a mental illness. But I found them meaningful and did not want the meaning dismissed. I decided to stop entering the trance states and interpreted them as God calling me to the ordained ministry.

As I felt vulnerable and did not want to fall victim to a religious cult, I went to an ancestral religious home, the Roman Catholic Church. Unable to reconcile confirming my faith as a Roman Catholic with the belief that I was called to ordination, I ended up confirming my faith as an Episcopalian. I remain something of a Catholic apologist, despite my issues with the

Church, and my involvement with other Protestant denominations.

Having graduated from Berkeley as a legal studies major, my first profession was as a legal assistant in Los Angeles and San Francisco. Working twelve-hour days six days a week, I crashed after a year on the job. What looked like over-achievement was a symptom of unrecognized, undiagnosed hypomania that came with a steep cost – my mental health and stability.

***

As a Working Adult

After working two years as a legal assistant, I quit, took time off, and applied for graduate school in psychology. While in graduate school, I worked as an administrator at a battered women's shelter and completed my field placement doing play therapy with severely emotionally disturbed children in day treatment.

June 1990, I got a Master of Arts in Psychology from New College of California. Over the next two years, I worked hard to rack up 3,000 internship hours. Then I studied for and passed the written and oral licensing exams. As there was a strong demand for psychotherapists in the non-profit sector to work with high-risk adolescents, that was where I found my jobs, working with teens: pregnant and parenting teens, and severely emotionally disturbed adolescents in residential and day treatment. That briefly summarizes my five-year career, from ages twenty-five to thirty, as a psychotherapist. Though my career was short-lived, it influenced how I think about mental health and mental illness. Above all else, it taught me compassion.

At thirty, I had a complete major depressive breakdown, found myself unable to get out of bed, and had to stop working. For the first time, I turned to a medical doctor for medication. Up until then, I had managed my depression with psychotherapy alone. My internist treated me first with fluoxetine (Prozac), the first Federal Drug Administration (FDA) approved selective serotonin reuptake inhibitor (SSRI). Fluoxetine overstimulated me and put me on edge. I felt as if an electric current ran through me and wanted to jump out of my skin. To take the edge off this side effect of fluoxetine, my doctor added trazodone, another antidepressant, which acts to balance serotonin in the brain.

My parents urged me to get a second opinion from a psychiatrist. Unfortunately, the psychiatrist I saw was old school and did not believe in using SSRIs, for there was no data as to the long-term consequences of using them. First, he took me off fluoxetine, prescribing only trazodone. Then he switched me to a tricyclic antidepressant, which led to ramping and cycling. Not only did the medication he prescribed cause me to spiral out of control, he told me that I was stuck at an adolescent stage of development. As I was an independent woman who had put herself through graduate school and supported herself living in the San Francisco Bay Area, I was insulted.

The tricyclic antidepressant triggered mania. I ended up spending a week awake, thinking simultaneously at rapid speed in binary (with ones and zeroes streaming through my mind), about chaos theory (which I had never studied), and about Christian mystics (with whom I strongly identify). At the time, I wished that there had been a way to record my thoughts so that later I could decipher them and see if any made sense. The content involved topics with which I had some basic knowledge and interest, but the experience was that of channeling information beyond my comprehension, way above my pay grade.

Having suffered a week of full-blown psychotic mania, I decided that I was not fit to be a psychotherapist. Though I clearly had a manic episode, I was not yet diagnosed as bipolar. Those who knew me at the time still find this fact shocking. Since the episode was likely precipitated by antidepressants, I was not prescribed a mood stabilizer. My psychiatrist prescribed a three-day regime of antipsychotics, which stopped the racing thoughts in their tracks, and allowed me to sleep.

After I had my breakdown at age thirty, I was unable to function on my own. I would fall asleep driving to my temporary job. When at the job, I couldn't even read. The words were all jumbled. However, I appeared competent. No one could see that I, a highly educated and articulate former professional woman, COULD NOT EVEN READ A SENTENCE.

To my parents' home and care I returned. They were tremendously supportive and encouraged my recovery. They gave me work to do around the house, and as my mental health improved, charged me room and board. The rent was more than I could earn doing odd jobs. We drew up a promissory note with well-defined terms, including interest charged for the money I owed them.

While living with my parents, I received psychiatric treatment and psychotherapy. My new psychiatrist carefully calibrated my dosage of sertraline (Zoloft), another SSRI. I remained stable on a low dose of sertraline for almost a decade, with a couple of trials of bupropion (Wellbutrin).

Once I was up for it, I got outside employment, starting as a temporary file clerk for a commercial real estate firm. What followed was a decade-long career in commercial real estate. It was a welcome change, not emotionally draining as helping severely emotionally disturbed youth, and it used my analytic and problem-solving skills. Still, I continued my pattern of overdoing it, working long hours and neglecting myself, leading to repeated burn out and cyclical depression. As a result, my résumé lists numerous short stints at various jobs and in multiple career areas. Three areas, really: legal assistant, psychotherapist, and commercial real estate professional. I worked short stints -- shooting high, crashing hard -- time and again.

Soon after moving back home and starting work as a temporary file clerk, I met my future husband, a civil engineer who didn't own a car, just three motorcycles and a small plane. Not your average engineer. Interesting. Complex. He even spoke Mandarin. Three years after we met, we married and later had a son. I found being home with an infant difficult. At the same time, I found being at work, away from him, heart-breaking.

***

As a Mother

Before becoming pregnant with my son, I thoroughly surveyed the medical research about antidepressant use in pregnancy and during lactation. Since I had a history of severe depression and suicidal ideation dating back to my late adolescence, I did not want the risk of experiencing depression during pregnancy. My review of scientific literature revealed that the antidepressant sertraline (Zoloft), an SSRI, had an extremely low serum level in breast milk, and an almost immeasurably low serum level in breast-feeding infants. Armed with this knowledge, and with my doctor's blessing, I took sertraline when I was pregnant and nursing my son. At the time, I received no negative feedback from health care providers, but I did get questions from extended family members, "Is it OK to breastfeed him when you are taking medicine?"

After childbirth, and a pregnancy that kept me bedridden for five weeks, I returned to the workplace on a part-time basis. My job, as always, grew, consuming more and more of my time, while my son needed me home with him. When I worked first two, then three days a week, my sister and my husband cared for my son. By the time my responsibilities demanded that I work four days a week until 7pm, I put my son in a loving, home-based childcare setting. Every time I would leave my son at childcare, he would cry for a good one and a half hours. I would visit him during my lunch hour, which meant that he would cry again after lunch. It broke my heart. Finally, I decided to quit work and stay home with him full-time. But, this too, would not last.

Staying home with my son full-time lasted a year and a half. By that time, the symptoms of hypomania returned. I thought that God was calling to one Episcopal Church for spiritual direction and another church for Bible study. Though God could have been calling me to these churches, this time I recognized the euphoria as hypomania. I could not in good conscience raise my son without treating symptoms of bipolar.

I asked my husband to listen in as I called the advice nurse and described my symptoms. She told me to either see a psychiatrist immediately or go to an emergency room. Unable to get seen by a psychiatrist for the first time on a Friday afternoon, I saw our family doctor who put me on divalproex sodium (seizure medication that acts as a mood stabilizer) with the understanding that it was outside her expertise and I was to see a psychiatrist following the weekend.

When I became a mother, I didn't know I had bipolar disorder. My diagnosis at the time was dysthymia (chronic depression). I knew I likely had, at the very least, cyclothymia (a mild form of bipolar disorder, also known as bipolar III). Once I got the diagnosis of bipolar disorder, my son was 27 months old and still nursing (he loved it and I was a pushover). I had to abruptly wean him, as the divalproex sodium (Depakote) I was prescribed as a mood stabilizer is not safe for nursing infants, or, in his case, a nursing toddler.

Fearing that I was now an unfit mother, I proceeded to put my son in day-care and reenter the workforce. Once my diagnosis changed from depression to bipolar, I believed that I could be a danger to my son and that he'd be better off in the care of someone else. I was the same person before my diagnosis changed. My stigma was internal: my own negative thoughts about what having bipolar meant, that I now had a serious, progressive mental illness, my belief that my son was no longer safe when in my own care. I was wrong. Despite the challenges of bipolar disorder -- and those challenges are real -- I'm a good mother. I work hard to be a good mother.

My son loved breastfeeding. He fed for twenty-seven months until it became clear that I was experiencing symptoms of hypomania and that I had bipolar disorder. To treat the manic symptoms, my doctor prescribed divalproex sodium (Depakote), an anticonvulsant commonly used as a mood stabilizer. Divalproex sodium is not recommended for use during pregnancy, for it may harm an unborn infant. This medication passes into breast milk. Consult your doctor before breast-feeding while taking this or any other medication.

Since divalproex sodium passes through breast milk, we agreed it was time to wean him. By this time my son was over two years old, and I was FED UP with waiting for him to "naturally" wean. Upon being prescribed divalproex sodium, I left my son with my husband for the weekend for cold turkey weaning while I went to my parents.

My son couldn't believe Mommy wasn't coming back home for the night. She had never left him overnight. Though it was raining, he insisted on sitting at the driveway, waiting for me to return, then my husband convinced him to sit under the walkway for cover from the rain, then sit in the front doorway, then at the foot of the stairs, then at the top of the stairs, then finally in the master bed with Daddy looking downstairs at the front door, until he finally fell asleep. Later, when I told this story to my psychotherapist, she found the story touching and indicative of how sensitive and caring my husband is.

The following week, I found a psychiatrist who would see me. Finally at the age of thirty-nine with a highly active, still nursing toddler son, I was diagnosed with bipolar disorder. I went back to work because I thought my son was better off in someone else's care, now that I was diagnosed with a chronic, severe, progressive, degenerative mental illness. I had internalized stigma against serious mental illness. For some reason, I thought it okay to be a depressed mom, but not a bipolar mom. I was the same person before and after the diagnosis. The only change was my treatment. Instead of only taking an antidepressant, now I was taking a mood stabilizer.

Keeping with my history of hypomanic workaholism, I worked increasingly long hours until I once again fell apart. I broke down crying at work and found myself unable to pull myself back together and return to the office. I tried taking a mental health week off but couldn't even make it through the weekend without succumbing to uncontrollable crying jags. To get myself stable, I had myself voluntarily hospitalized when my son was four and haven't returned to work since.

***

Acceptance

Acceptance has been an ongoing process for me. Not just overcoming denial or stigma but owning my diagnosis and allowing others in to help me. I had been a high achiever, a perfectionist. Accepting that I have a mental illness has involved accepting myself as broken, as imperfect, as fallible, as human.

To that extent, acceptance has allowed me to forgive myself for not living up to early life expectations. I quit UCLA after my freshman year. Took a semester off. Attended community college part-time before transferring to UC Berkeley. I never became a doctor or a lawyer. But I did get my bachelor's, a master's in psychology, and much later even attended seminary twice after my hospitalization, but never finished my religious studies.

That I attended seminary twice AFTER I had been hospitalized indicates that my sense of calling never quite died. The psychologist I saw after my hospitalization asked me about my sense of calling. She had been raised in a convent by nuns, so she understood what I meant by sensing that I had a calling, a higher purpose, that maybe I was supposed to go to seminary and preach. That feeling had been validated over the years. I had been told that I had a gift for preaching.

At times, I was shocked that I could persuade people in debates. I enjoyed the challenge of debating the "wrong" side of an issue and convincing people that what I argued was true (even when it was clearly wrong). In junior high, I persuaded the class that we had been visited by aliens. Whether or not we have been, our scientific evidence of such a visit is lacking. In high school, as Scarlett O'Hara in a theatrical debate, I convinced the class that slavery was right. It's NOT! That I can convince people of falsehoods scares me.

Similarly, given my history of mental illness, I've questioned my sense of religious calling, and whether I was suited for ordination and pastoral ministry. Still, after my psychiatric hospitalization, which I discussed openly with my pastor, he recommended me for seminary. I attended part-time for a year. While at Fuller Seminary, I wrote a Mental Health Ministry manual. As I explored what my calling was, it became clear that I was called to a mental health ministry.

My studies went well until we moved to Eugene, Oregon. The move to a rainy, overcast climate amid pines that block the sun, triggered a depressive episode during which I slept throughout the day, and had to set an alarm to pick my son up from school. I withdrew from seminary and focused on my mental health recovery.

We decided to move back to California – what my Eugene psychiatrist called the "geographic cure" – for my mental health. Later, when stable, I reapplied to seminary, this time to study theology for a career in academics, rather than my previous studies in divinity for ordination as a pastor. I did well academically and enjoyed studying Hebrew. Then the recession hit, my husband lost his job, and we had to move to the Mojave Desert for employment. When I decided to withdraw, Fuller Seminary reached out to me to offer financial assistance. I explained that the issue wasn't just financial – the stress of unemployment and moving made it untenable for me to continue my studies. I tried to continue my religious studies online, but found that overwhelming when struggling with bipolar depression.

Now, I don't even go to church. My husband and I talk about attending local small congregations, but end up cocooning on Sundays. When I become involved in group activities, like attending church, I get overstimulated, overwhelmed, and overextended. I tend to volunteer to do too much. I do better with solitude. Praying alone or with my husband. Both my religious and mental health recovery journeys have led to acceptance. Acceptance is essentially a spiritual experience. Whatever your faith, whether you believe in a higher purpose, to accept yourself is to love yourself.

I am not weak. I am vulnerable. I am not perfect and flawless. I am loved, lovable, and loving. My life has meaning. My life experience gives me purpose in helping others. I am grateful that I can write and speak to share my journey with others, hoping that it inspires others to accept themselves.

***

How I Cope

My treatment regimen and coping skills have evolved over time. At 18-years-old, I sought help at UCLA's student health services. The cognitive therapy I got there helped me to identify my suicidal thoughts, stop them, and rewrite them into more rational thoughts. That skill stays with me to this day. In my twenties, I studied and sought therapy that explored the effects that alcoholism and family dynamics had on me.

Then at thirty, as a psychotherapist of severely emotionally disturbed teens, following the deaths of my grandmother and a friend from high school, I fell into a depression so deep that psychotherapy alone was not enough. From then on, I needed medication to maintain my mental health. Until I was thirty-nine, I remained stable on antidepressant medication and psychotherapy. At that point, experiencing elation and intrusive religious thoughts, I knew I was hypomanic and needed psychiatric treatment for bipolar disorder. From that point on, I've been treated by psychiatrists who have medicated me for bipolar disorder, a brain disorder which requires daily mood stabilizing medication. Medication treats, but does NOT cure, the underlying brain disorder. I still experience symptoms of bipolar disorder, albeit milder. Living well with bipolar means I must attend psychotherapy, use my hard-earned insight and arsenal of coping skills, and exercise self-care.

Honestly, it's taken decades for me to develop excellent coping skills. I've always been good at asking for help and getting support from friends and family. My social skills have helped me to surround myself with loving and supportive friends and family. I'm honest and open about my symptoms and what support I need at the time.

That may mean that I have my husband get take-out or make dinner when I'm wiped out and not up to the task. I rely on my husband quite a bit. No doubt his role as my caregiver is tough. We are partners and help each other, but I make sure I express my gratitude for all he does.

I make sure I get a good night's sleep every night. Regular sleep is essential to good mental health, especially when living with bipolar disorder. Every night before I go to bed, to quiet my mind, I read on a tablet using a dark screen with warm-tinted text. If racing thoughts keep me awake, I listen to a mindfulness app sleep story, or two or three. If that doesn't work, I take medications approved and/or prescribed by my psychiatrist. I MUST silence those hypomanic racing thoughts to sleep.

I do what I can, when I can. I've learned to lower my expectations of myself. I change my mind. I cancel plans. I drop out of classes. I avoid commitments. "Failure" is always an option. I redefine what success looks like. I reject the need to be productive.

Some of the coping skills that work for me wouldn't work for you. I avoid deadlines, for I ramp up to workaholic hypomania when faced with a deadline, especially when I'm working for someone else. You may have to meet deadlines for your job.

To manage my "To Do" list, I use my cell phone's calendar app. I schedule modest goals. If I can't complete a task, I reschedule, revise, reconsider, or delete it.

Not only do deadlines trigger hypomania in me, so do crowds, conferences, and loud noises. I avoid overstimulating triggers. I keep all social media notifications off. I pop in and out as suits my needs.

At times, it may appear as if I'm isolating, but I prefer solitude and find cocooning peaceful. Besides, unless I leave my house, I'm never alone, for I'm married and have an 19-year-old son living at home.

Years of therapy have given me insight. I'm aware of stressors that may make my mood go up or down. I avoid caffeine after noon. Screen phone calls. Write out thoughts that clutter my mind. During the day I write, blog, and use social media to connect with others in the mental health community.

Humor is a fabulous coping skill, both for me personally, and for my husband and me in our marriage.

***

Successes, Hopes, & Dreams

To live successfully with bipolar, I've learned to be flexible. When I fall, when my journey is interrupted, I reassess and adapt. When I quit UCLA, I took a semester off and then went to community college before transferring to Berkeley. I had hoped to become a doctor, a neurosurgeon. That hope, that dream, that goal changed. I learned that I must take life as it comes, adjusting my goals as needed.

When I fell into a deep depression, and later a week of mania, I couldn't return to work right away. I decided not to return to my profession as a psychotherapist, took time off, and then worked in a temporary job, which led to a decade-long career in commercial real estate.

When recovering from my breakdown, at what would seem to be my lowest point, I met my future husband. We married and had a child. We've been together now twenty-five years, married for twenty-two years. My baby boy is now a 19-year-old young man. My greatest success has been being a loving wife and mother.

My mental health journey has led me here, now. I am a well-respected mental health advocate, active online and in my local community. My success includes publishing this book and the writing I've done online.

Writing is therapeutic, allowing me to organize my thoughts. When I speak in person (not as a public speaker, but in person socially), I lack impulse control and don't always say the "right" or politic thing. I basically speak my mind with no filter. When I write, my words are honest, but more carefully chosen. The act of writing slows me down, giving my jumbled thoughts a place to go. Then I rewrite and rewrite and rewrite. In rewriting, I organize, and I reframe those thoughts. It's a cognitive exercise, retelling a story, reframing it, re-examining it. The story changes as we change, as our perception changes.

Now I'm getting requests to speak about my mental health journey. I've always hoped to be a public speaker, which I've done through organizations like the National Association on Mental Illness (NAMI) and the International Bipolar Foundation (IBPF). My training in high school as a drama geek, in seminary, and with NAMI has prepared me to realize this dream, this hope, this goal.

Right now, I'm living my dream by writing my story, by sharing it here in this book and on my blog, by telling my story aloud to others. I had hoped to be a published author and public speaker, and now I am. I have more to say. More to write. This is a beginning for me, yet another beginning.

My hopes and dreams for the future are continued public education about mental illness, overcoming stigma and discrimination, and better research and treatment for brain disorders. Much of my mental health advocacy is sharing information about the latest scientific research about brain health. I'm a science geek at heart. I will continue to share content from sources like the National Institute of Mental Health and the Brain and Behavior Research Foundation.

BIPOLAR THOUGHTS

The Outsider

As some of you may know, I struggle with bipolar disorder. I'm impetuous, speaking without thinking. I feel compelled to say what others won't. And, by pointing out the elephant in the room, what is clearly obvious, but no one dares state, I pay for it. I once again offend, infuriate, and alienate those I love. That is my role, the role of an outsider.

***

Titrating Stimulation

Find I must titrate exposure to stimulation. Need enough to prevent depression, but not so much as to trigger hypomania. Enough, but not too much sun. Must be very careful with social stimulation. Easily get on edge when I spend too much time with too many people. And, not able to limit myself, to set boundaries, to keep myself on an even keel. Fear losing myself, jumping in too deep too soon, taking on more than I can handle. All a very careful balancing act.

***

Grief, Anxiety, and Hypomania

So, what brought on this flurry of activity, this bout of defensive hypomania, the birth of this blog now? Two things: one, I forgot to take valproic acid Thursday night, and, two, my grief in facing my father-in-law's health crisis. Writing is one way I can deal with my grief, the pain I am feeling, and the compassion and empathy I feel for my husband, his mother, and everyone else in our extended clan who are hoping and praying that my father-in-law will recover from sepsis.

***

Siren Song

I have heard the siren song of alcohol and marijuana. Craved the quieting of my thoughts, the slowing down. Prescribed medications help immensely, but I still understand and am wary of alcohol's hold on me. I have that propensity to become an alcoholic. I can sense it in me, and fear it.

When my father-in-law was admitted into the ICU recently, I went out and bought myself a six-pack of light beer. Told myself that I was just drinking a little, just one bottle of light beer each night, but I craved more. The feeling of intoxication wasn't strong enough, didn't last long enough. I metabolized its effects way too quickly and was left unsatisfied, wanting more. After finishing the six-pack over the course of six nights, I bought myself a bottle of wine. Red wine is good for me, I told myself, all while knowing that I was drinking to numb myself, even if briefly and mildly. I realize that one bottle of beer a night may not qualify me as an alcoholic, but its hold on me does put me at risk. I poured out the bottle of wine as I spoke on the phone with a close friend.

Alcohol can damage our livers, our brains, and our relationships. It's especially not good in combination with medication for mood disorders, intensifying those medications' negative side effects as well as the effect of alcohol. The mood stabilizer valproic acid, or Depakote, can damage the liver, one reason why our doctors have us get labs done regularly. Antidepressants negatively interact with alcohol, as well. So, I should steer clear of alcohol.

Pot, I stopped smoking over twenty-five years ago under doctor orders when I was severely depressed. My doctor chided me, telling me that I know marijuana is a central nervous system depressant, and that I should know better than to smoke it. I was a mental health professional at the time, counseling teens, no less, so I did know better. On my doctor's advice, I quit. Still, even to this day, if I smell it, I crave it. When I was in my twenties and diagnosed depressed but not bipolar, back before I sought medical help for my illness, when I relied on therapy alone, marijuana slowed me down and made me stupid. A huge relief. I could not slow my thoughts down on my own. Pot gave my mind rest. I do support the legalization and regulation of marijuana, and do believe that it has beneficial medical uses when prescribed under the treatment and supervision of a responsible and knowledgeable medical doctor.

***

Obsessive Thoughts

We never really know the content of others' thoughts, if they think in the same way as we do, in words, conversation, images, or impulses. When I was in my twenties, I sought and received psychotherapy for depression, but didn't know I had bipolar disorder. High achievers, those with racing thoughts and workaholic leanings, were not diagnosed as bipolar back in the '80s and early '90s. We maintained a facade of normalcy. We held jobs, had stable relationships, paid our bills, stayed out of trouble. As I achieved, as I maintained the illusion of mental health and stability, I struggled with disturbing thoughts and impulses that made no sense.

One day while waiting for the BART train in San Francisco, I found my-self with an unsettling intrusive thought, image and impulse. For no rea-son whatsoever, I felt compelled to push a stranger in front of the train. I thought the thought, saw an image of myself pushing the stranger in front of the train, felt the impulse to do so, and had to argue with myself re-strain myself to prevent me from doing so. I told myself, "You feel no anger toward this person. Even if you *were* angry, it is wrong to push people in front of trains. It is murder. If you pushed that person in front of the train, he would die." I felt no murderous rage. Absolutely no feeling attached itself to the thought, the image, the impulse. Yet, I had to struggle with myself, hold an unseen internal debate, rein in the impulse. I wondered if other people had similar thoughts, similar impulses, and if so, why weren't people getting pushed in front of trains all the time. Because I was working really hard not to do so, for that action was extremely ego dystonic for me. I saw myself as a good, helpful, loving person, not a killer.

When driving over bridges or on windy mountainous roads, I've had sim-ilar impulses, and had to argue, "Kitt, you cannot fly. If you drove off this bridge/cliff, you would die. You do not want to die. You would devastate many people - friends, family, suicidal psychotherapy clients - if you did so. Stop. Stay on this road, on this bridge, do not drive off it."

Then there have been lesser impulses with associated images of me hang-ing up the phone mid-conversation for no reason, seeing myself throwing plates without any of the passionate fury usually connected with that act.

Never have I come close to killing anyone, nor have I driven off any bridge or cliff. I do understand, though, what it is like to have unsettling impulses and thoughts. For me, those impulses and thoughts conflict with my sense of self, my ability to reason, my internal moral compass.

Under different circumstances, fueled by rage, not compulsion, I have broken a couple of plates and slammed a few doors. I am a fiery Irish lass, after all.

***

Living in My Head

I live my life in my head, in thoughts, in daydreams. My thirteen-year-old son, sitting next to me in the car, sees me gesturing to my internal monologue and urges, "Mom, stop it. Live your life." When I daydream, I am not living in the present. I must practice mindfulness and remember to be here now.

Mindfulness practices that sometimes help me include meditation, but other times my rapid thoughts cannot be silenced.

Prayer, open-ended contemplative prayer, which is a form of meditation, often helps. I simply think, "Dear God…" and open my heart, sharing my burdens with God.

To fall asleep, I once listened to relaxation recordings, guided mediations geared towards relaxing the body and mind. Now, I find listening to sleep stories (Sleep Stories by Calm app) more relaxing. Listening to the bedtime stories, my mind is distracted from my thoughts; instead, I'm immersed in other relaxing worlds.

Going outside and getting closer to nature helps, even if that means just looking at the sky or flowers growing in the neighborhood. Walking gets me out of my head and grounds me in the physical world.

Sometimes, I simply take a deep breath.

***

Mind Slog

Depakote (valproic acid) dosage increased. Thoughts slowed way down. Now slogging through my mind. Inspiration gone. Where is my muse? Know I needed to slow down, to catch my breath. Know this increased dose is temporary, that my mind will work better, quicker soon, after a month or two. Goal is to stabilize and then go back to my usual mainte-nance dose. Anything, any little thing, or now a big emotional stressor, can and will set me off on a roller coaster of moods. Now is the time to regain composure. What feels like stasis will lead to balance. Take a deep breath and relax.

***

Mosaic Tile Shelf

My son designed a mosaic tile shelf that I recently made. Having ordered a box of random broken Talavera tile, I ended up with a lot of yellow tile. Apparently yellow was not as popular as other colors. My son and I looked at the tile array and he suggested sun and sky. It mirrors our view of Saddleback, the two highest peaks in the Santa Ana Mountains. The day dawning over the hills symbolizes hope for the future. I'm not able to find words to express that hope right now, not because I am depressed, but because I am struggling to string words together to form complete sentences or complex thoughts. This post is an exercise in writing despite the slow, lethargic state of my mind. Look forward to going back down to my maintenance dose of Depakote (valproic acid). This is very frustrating and exhausting.

Hunger and Headaches

Now that I'm on a higher dose of Depakote (valproic acid), I'm always hungry and have a headache. I cannot satiate my hunger, and I tire of popping ibuprofens to relieve the dull ache in my forehead. My body has adjusted somewhat to the increased dosage, no longer struggling to stay awake during the day, yet requiring sleep meds to fall asleep at night. My mind, though not as slow, grasps for the right word and stumbles over nouns.

***

Back to the Mundane

As my mind has slowed, I've gone from prolific blog writing to playing solitaire on my iPad. Back to the inane, the mundane. Not as creative, but better able to take care of daily routines, pay bills, follow up on paperwork, go grocery shopping. Exhausted, though, and not up to cooking complete meals. Heated up frozen taquitos for dinner the other night, fast food last night, pizza tonight. Getting tired of the lethargy. Want and need more pep.

***

To Conform or Not to Conform

I always have had a beef with conformity, with hiding your authentic self to fit in with the crowd. Why not be brave and be yourself? Why not be different? Isn't that what makes life interesting?

As I have aged, though, I still am very much Kitt, I find I have more in common with others than not. Our differences are primarily superficial. Of course, my struggles with bipolar disorder are not universally shared, but we as humans all love and desire to be loved. We have families. We have friends. We protect our young and mourn loss.

To the extent that we differ, we should, we must, respect and appreciate those differences. We are all deserving of love, of acceptance.

Bottom line: I am Kitt, my personality exists independent of my illness. I am a unique individual, whether or not I have bipolar disorder. You and I, every living being, are both unique and alike. Paradoxical, but true. We are individuals with unique personalities. We are also human, with similar needs and desires. We are all more alike than different. To the extent that we are alike, let's show compassion. To the extent that we are different, let's strive for understanding and acceptance.

***

Aftermath of Suicide

When in the throes of suicidal ideation, you don't, and often can't, understand suicide's negative effects on those left behind. When I was eighteen, I thought my loved ones would be better off without me. My suicidal ideation was so entrenched, it was ego syntonic. It agreed with my sense of self, my way of perceiving myself in relation to the world. Not until I was a thirty-year-old psychotherapist, did I realize how devastating and harmful the act of suicide, specifically my own suicide, would be on others. I knew that at the very least, I would have harmed my clients. How could I help depressed, abused, or abandoned adolescent clients by succumbing to depression and taking my own life? I understood that taking my life would devastate my clients, and from that I could reason my death would also devastate those who knew and loved me. By then, my rational self knew that I was loved and that my actions affected those I loved. My suicidal ideation had finally become ego dystonic, in conflict with my sense of self, with a more rational thought process, and with my better understanding of human feelings, thoughts and behaviors. Helping others enabled me to take a step back and see myself as I saw my clients, to have more compassion for myself.

* * *

Ticket to Work

This week I signed up for Social Security's Ticket to Work program (ssa.gov/work/). The program is designed to transition those of us receiving disability back into the workplace. I am doing so with trepidation, for the last time I worked, I overworked, pushed myself beyond my limits and ended up in the hospital. To re-enter the workforce in a sustainable manner I must take manageable steps, wading into the waters, not diving too deep too soon.

Thursday morning, I had my first job interview in more than a decade. The next day a Ticket to Work service provider recommended that I revise my résumé, tailoring it to the part-time administrative positions I am seeking. They also referred me to online resources to update my software skills.

I could use prayers and encouragement as I set off on this journey back to work. Thank you.

***

What to do?

Freaking out, ramping up, as I begin my part-time job search.

Reminded:

> *"Just because you can, doesn't mean you should."*
> *- Christina Harrington*

***

Slowing It Down

Slowing it down, breaking it down into manageable bite-size tasks. Put off job search for now. Became overwhelmed. Feared hypomania, mixed episodes, and eventual hospitalization. Feared job taking over, not being able to set limits, boundaries. My permeable self, the self that enables me to empathize, is too soft. Not able to say No or Later or When I Can Get to It. Not able to delegate. Take on too much. Feel sucked in. And, then I leave, flee, escape. Cocoon myself at home. Hide.

Adolescent client once said my heart is too soft.

For now, I start going to my psychiatrist's group therapy sessions. Signed up for a writing workshop, always afraid of overstimulation; still, not sure what I can do, how much I can do and remain stable. Signed up for Zumba Gold class once a week. Daily, take care of husband and son. Dogs looking at me for attention, following me around, sleeping at my feet. In the master bed now, writing, using computer and Google calendar to organize my life.

***

Freaking Out

Both my husband and my mother have expressed concern that I am ramping up (becoming hypomanic and experiencing mixed emotional states) as I've started the Ticket to Work process. I have had trouble sleeping, my mind is racing, I'm anxious, and I've shed a few tears. I put in a call to my psychiatrist. Both my mom and my husband think I should start more modestly, perhaps volunteering or taking an art class.

Whenever I take a step outside the structure, responsibilities, and expectations of my family life, and try to take on some other activity, I become overwhelmed and start to fall apart. It doesn't take much to destabilize me,

I'm kind of freaking out.

***

Flurries of Hypomania

Or, is it just that I had iced tea yesterday with my lunch?

Since I've been mildly hypomanic, I enrolled in my psychiatrist's therapy group to see what happens to me when I am in a social situation. For me, social stimulation can trigger hypomania, anxiety, and mood cycling.

Or, maybe it's just that time of year. Spring is coming. The birds are chirping. Trees are throwing out their pollen. The daffodils already came and went in the warmth of Southern California.

***

Freestyling It

Neither line dancing nor Zumba are for me. Don't enjoy doing the same thing, the same way at the same time as everyone else. Goes against my nature. I'm more of a free-style dancer, mixing up my moves, varying dance styles, dancing with the beat, then at double beat, then slowly to the melody. Never one for convention.

***

Grounded by the Flu

The whole family got the stomach flu. Grounded me. Slowed me down. On the positive side, I caught up on sleep and am on a more even keel. Not hypomanic as long as I feel this fatigued. Not as productive, either. At least my mind is at rest -- for now.

***

Forgot to Take Meds

Last night I forgot to take my Depakote (actually, I take generic Divalproex). I was tossing and turning in bed with racing thoughts and the impulse to write and edit. Finally, I took Sonata (once again, I take the generic version, but I do not recall the generic name) and fell asleep. This morning, I went to take my morning medication (escitalopram, generic for Lexapro) and saw that I had neglected to take last night's dose of Divalproex. Well, no wonder I was hypomanic, had racing thoughts, and could not fall asleep. I need to take my mood stabilizer; without it my moods are, quite honestly, unstable. I hate it when I forget a dose. I am so sensitive biochemically; one missed dose can really throw me off.

***

On Edge

On edge

Fingers shaking

Irritable

Prickly

Damn, what one missed med dose can do to one's body

***

Postpartum

Thoughts and urges

Never disclosed

Never shared

Until now

Little baby boy

Pretty rose between his legs

So pretty

Want to take him in my mouth

So yummy

Want to eat him up

Unsettling urges

No rhyme or reason

Thoughts that pass

Memory remains

Urges not actions

Sti l disturbing

Is this what it means?

"So cute, I could eat him up!"

Nc desire

Nc emotions

Behind the thoughts

Behind the urges

Just disturbing thoughts

Fleeting compulsions

To eat a baby boy

***

Not Just Dysthymia

Not until I was thirty-nine, was I diagnosed as having bipolar disorder. I am now fifty. At thirty-nine, I recognized the symptoms of mania in myself, euphoria, the feeling of being called by God to a particular church, to a particular path. The diagnostic criteria have changed over the years. For two decades, I had been diagnosed and treated as dysthymic, or pervasively and chronically depressed. I would tell my physicians that I was probably at the very least cyclothymic, experiencing a pattern of higher highs and lower lows than is the norm, that I was far more productive than most people, that I moved and thought faster, did more, exhausted myself, and burned out on a regular periodic basis.

***

To Work or Not to Work

My experience has been that in the workplace I become overstimulated, that I take on too many responsibilities, overwork, and burn out. Taking care of my husband and son, as well as myself, taxes me as it is. I need social contact, but still feel that it must be restrained, limited, flexible to my needs and the needs of my family. Group therapy as well as the writers' workshops that I have begun attending give me needed structure and stimulation. They enable me to rejoin the world outside my home, away my family room couch where I sit in front of the TV until it's once again time to pick up my son or go grocery shopping. These group activities provide me with a sense of accomplishment and competence. Unlike a job, where there are multiple, competing priorities and deadlines, I am not asked to perform. Unlike taking a position as administrative assistant for which I am overqualified, I am learning from those more qualified and experienced than I.

***

LMFT

Back in 1990, I got an MA in psychology from New College of California. I worked hard over the next two years to rack up the then required 3,000 internship hours, and study for and pass both the written and oral exams to become what was then called a Marriage, Family, and Child Counselor. The license has since been renamed Marriage and Family Therapist.

As I specialized in counseling adolescents, the former license name better described what I did. While in grad school, a school that offered a master's, not a doctorate, my Child Psychology instructor told me that I could not make it professionally as a child therapist, that to get clients one must do psychological testing, the domain of psychologists.

I was enraged. She was wrong. There was a strong demand for psychotherapists in the non-profit sector to work with high-risk adolescents. Upon graduation, that was where I found my jobs, working with teens: pregnant and parenting teens, and severely emotionally disturbed adolescents in residential and day treatment.

That's my "ancient" history, my short-lived profession practiced when I was in my mid-twenties to age thirty. As I mentioned before, at thirty I had a complete psychiatric breakdown, was literally unable to get out of bed, and had to stop working. From that time on, I maintained my license, paying the necessary fees, and when the licensing board offered an inactive designation, I maintained my license on an inactive basis.

May 2014, my still inactive license comes up for renewal, and I'm faced with the question: should I keep my California Marriage and Family Therapist license inactive, or should I take the continuing education credits and activate my license?

What would I do with my license? I can see myself doing education. I can see myself leading groups. Not so sure about individual, couples, or family psychotherapy. I would need to be careful in protecting myself. And then there's the cost of rent and professional liability insurance.

As the time to renew approaches, another week goes by, and I am leaning towards taking the continuing education credits to activate my license. Interesting note, I see myself more as a "former" psychotherapist than a "former" commercial real estate professional, although I worked in commercial real estate for twice as many years. In part, I believe it is because I was educated as a psychotherapist. My graduate education, internships, written and oral exams, as well as continuing education, weekly supervision, case conferences, and a lifetime of dealing with mental health issues.

This post has been sitting as a draft since last week. Now I'm thinking that I will renew my license as inactive and activate it when the time seems right. Quite ambivalent. Next week I have signed up for a webinar hosted by the International Bipolar Foundation entitled "E-Mental Health: Computer and Device Assisted Therapies for Mental Illnesses." The topic intrigues me. Using the internet as an interface may provide me with what I need to maintain professional distance. Who knows? I guess I'll learn more about the subject next Thursday.

***

Another Late Night

A couple nights ago, or perhaps it was simply last night, I was up late, unable to fall asleep. Finally, at 1:30 am, I decided to check if I had taken my nighttime meds (generic Depakote aka Divalproex aka valproic acid and generic Benadryl aka long chemical name I do not care to look up). Turns out I had not, so I did so, and added a clonazepam which I chewed to ensure rapid drowsiness.

Tonight, I'm again up late. This night I took my meds. The stimulation of group therapy followed by a writer's group has me tired but very much awake. My body wants sleep, my mind is not ready to let go. Debating whether to take a clonazepam or simply lay down, close my eyes, and relax. Maybe I'll just continue reading the book of one of the writers I have recently met. My reading list has grown since I've started associating with writers.

***

Day-Tripping

Often, I get caught in my thoughts, in daydreaming and talking to myself, even gesturing and making facial expressions to match my train of thought. Keeps me from being in the present and drives my son nuts, especially when I do it driving him to and from school.

My hope is to get those thoughts out and onto this blog. My plan is to start vlogging my daydreams, perhaps as streams of consciousness. Haven't yet set up a camera to do so. Tried my iPhone in the car, but when I mounted it on the dashboard, it obscured my field of vision, which, of course, is dangerous.

Organizing My Thought Process

Tuesday in group therapy, my psychiatrist pointed out that when sharing in group therapy, I talk around my point until I finally get to it. Unlike my writing, which is usually terse and to the point, my speech (at least in therapy, where I allow myself freer rein than in my daily life where I mostly listen to, or feign interest in, my husband and son, and keep my own rambling and often narcissistic thoughts to myself in the form of ongoing oratorical daydreams) -- now back to the thought thread -- my speech reflects my thought process. He recommended that I start organizing my speech and thereby my thought process. Interesting observation. Perhaps participating in Toastmasters, which has been on my To Do list for years, and is even scheduled weekly in my calendar, will help me do just that: organize my thought process, pare it down, slow it down. Unlike much of my blog posts, where I somewhat purposefully write in a more disorganized fashion with parentheses and such. Convoluted and all over the place, like my thought process.

***

Crap

Crap. Forgot to collect mail from mailbox for three days this week. Bills now in a pile, including a paperwork nightmare in which our medical insurance is denying claims retroactively. Mind on edge. Caffeine or something else. Hypomania, perhaps. Definitely irritable, and something close to anxious. As if something is about to change. Could be I'm simply anxious about visiting my parents. Worried about them. That's probably part of it. Also trying to get some loose ends taken care of. House projects completed. Happy to see bathroom walls finally repaired. Soon the rooms will look great. The bathrooms, that is. The rest of the house remains partially painted with unpacked boxes waiting for finished rooms.

***

Overcast

This morning I struggled to keep my eyes open as I drove my son to school. No more searing heat, Santa Ana winds, and fire. May gloom is here. We need the coolness. We need rain. Unfortunately, when the sun hides, I find it difficult to stay awake. When we moved to Eugene, I had to set an alarm to pick my son up from school. Remaining awake and alert when driving was a daily struggle in the damp and cloudy Northwest. Here in Southern California, I have a better time of it, but today I struggle.

***

Irritable

Irritable

Headachy

Not sleepy and it's late

Been bitchy

Too critical

On the rag

Approaching menopause

Mean

Had a couple of days of clouds

Of gloom

Slept

Now this

Irritated

Change again

Back to sunny

Too soon

Too much

Cannot take it

Make up your fucking mind

What is it?

***

Screwed Up

Both yesterday and today I screwed up my meds. When I got ready for bed last night, I saw that I hadn't yet taken my morning dose of escitalopram oxalate (Lexapro). Then this morning after I took my morning meds, I noticed that both my morning and evening doses were gone. I had taken both. Crap. I do have a system: two pill holders, one light transparent green for the morning, one light transparent blue for the evening, but the colors are similar and pill box shapes identical. Maybe I need to be able to more clearly differentiate between the two. I'm fighting sleep right now, not because of weather, for it is sunny, but because I took my night-time dose of divalproex (Depakote) and diphenhydramine (Benadryl).

***

The Rebel and His Mother

The Rebel

When my son was a preschooler in daycare

His class had a field trip to the local In 'N Out

As we walked back to the daycare center

My son held my hand

We walked in pairs down the sidewalk

45

His daycare teacher said

Everyone, stay on the sidewalk

Do not step into the driveway or the road

My three-year old son touched his foot in the gutter

Just his tippy toe

His teacher swiftly grabbed him from my hands

Took him with her to the front of the line

She gave me another child to walk

A more compliant, less rebellious child

My son, he was rewarded

He got to walk at the front of the line

Beside his favorite teacher

I was punished

Humiliated actually

Bad mother

Cannot control her child

Later that day when I returned to work

I told this story

One of my bosses smiled

Kitt, you love that in your boy

That your boy rebels against the rules

Just like the Berkeley rabble-rouser you once were

Pushing the limits

Yes, it still brings a smile to my face

That I have a son who dared touch his toe to the gutter

He understood the importance of staying with the group

He understood the spirit of the law

He did not run out into the road

Yet he questioned, dared to test, the letter of the law

What happens, he wondered, if I break this rule just a little bit

The memory also hurts

How dare that teacher rip my son from my hand

How dare she judge me and my child

Deem me unfit to walk my son back to daycare

Before I had to return to work

Return to work judged an ineffective mother

Return to work rather than stay with my son

Now that I think about it

He punished me

How dare I go back to work

How dare I not stay home with him

His Mother

This event happened more than sixteen years ago, and it still sears my memory. I was not feeling very confident in my parenting skills at the time. From the expressions on the other parents' faces, I could tell that they were shocked at her treatment of me. I complained to the daycare center director, and the teacher lost her job. I ater regretted having complained because although she lacked adult social skills, the kids loved her and re-sponded well to her structure. My son loved this teacher a great deal. She ended up being his after-school teacher at his pre-kindergarten school, and we later hired her to babysit him in her own apartment, which was a treat for him. She irked the administration and her co-workers at her next job, as well. She was great with preschoolers, but you do not treat an adult like a preschooler.

A year later, when my son was four, I fell apart, crying hysterically in the parking lot of my employer, and ended up voluntarily hospitalizing myself. I had put my son in daycare because I thought my son would be better off in someone else's hands. I was afraid of my temper and my mood swings. I was afraid I might hurt my son. I like to think of my hospitalization as God teaching me otherwise. My illness made it so that I had to stay home with my son, who, as it turned out, needed me home. Choosing to believe that I was meant to stay home with my son, and that my illness forced me to do so, is my way of positively reframing my experience of mothering with bipolar disorder. I choose to positively embrace my two-week stay in the hospital, months of partial hospitalization, and subsequent enrollment on disability. I simply was unable to balance work with mothering while living with bipolar disorder. I am no super woman. I am a mother with bipolar disorder doing the best that she can.

Ever since my hospitalization nine years ago, I've been home on disability. This past February, I initiated a job search and considered re-entering the work force. As I applied for jobs and went on interviews, I started ramping up, became hypomanic, and panicked at the thought of returning to work. I feared ending up once again overwhelmed and hospitalized. Since then I have focused on blogging, participating in group therapy, and attending two weekly writing groups. My son says I'm addicted to blogging and to using social media. Perhaps. But it feels good. I'm impassioned. It's about time!

***

Bad Mom

Bad mom

Selfish mom

Ineffective mom

Permissive mom

Bipolar mom

At times, abusive mom

At times, out of control mom

At times, rageful mom

She's even hit her kid

She's even slapped her kid

No excuse

No excuse to hit a child

No excuse to slap a child

At my son's request, I revised this poem, comments, and replies. My son would have preferred that I delete the poem entirely. Since I think that explosive anger and loss of control when disciplining a child are important issues to address, I am taking ownership of my behavior and not sharing his behavior. He was, after all, a minor, and he deserves respect and privacy.

Though an accurate description of my behavior on more than one occasion, this poem is not the whole story. I like to think that I am, or at least I try to be, a devoted loving mother.

***

Suicide Infanticide

Long, long ago

When my son was very, very young

I thought of killing myself

But what about my son?

I can't leave him behind

Well then, I'll take him with me

Oh, my God!

That's where it comes from

That's why mothers take their children's lives

When depressed and suicidal

They do not want to abandon their children

They do not want to leave them behind

It's not rational

It's a depressed and suicidal thought process

That takes a leap

From killing oneself

To killing the one most cherished

I get it now

I get it

My brain went there

There

To that completely unacceptable place

I considered killing both myself and my son

The thought was momentary

It came

It left

The thought happened long, long ago

But it did happen

I did think it

Thank God I recognized my thoughts as irrational

Thank God I had done so much work in therapy

Thank God I was on antidepressants

Or, maybe, not

Maybe the antidepressants

Hormonal changes of birth and breastfeeding

Lack of uninterrupted sleep

Triggered these thoughts

During my son's infancy, I was not diagnosed bipolar. Diagnostic criteria did not yet describe people like me. I would tell doctors that I was probably at the very least cyclothymic. To my family doctor, wife of a psychiatrist, I had depression and responded well to antidepressants. Researching antidepressants before I became pregnant, I chose Zoloft, an SSRI deemed safe for pregnant and breastfeeding women. So, I took Zoloft during pregnancy and while breastfeeding.

Antidepressants can trigger hypomania, mania, even psychosis in those of us with bipolar disorder. Treatment (even with lithium, mood stabilizers, and/or antipsychotics) does not guarantee an absence of symptoms, including depressed or suicidal thoughts, mania, hypomania, or mixed states. Living with a mental illness requires diligence, self-awareness, and knowledge.

***

Ramping Up

Have not been falling asleep on my own recently. Have had to drug myself, dosing myself with a combination of clonazepam, diphenhydramine (Benadryl), and an herbal supplement sleep aid. I chew the clonazepam and herbal supplement to get them to act more rapidly.

Find myself up until the wee hours of the morning, intermittently reading eBooks and blog posts, commenting on blog posts, responding to comments on my posts, researching any number of things that come to mind. One thing leads to another. Read something that I must then write about or research. Mind all over the place. Mind thinking. Not tired. Crap. At least taking the clonazepam knocks me out. Wait too long until I take it. Well, maybe 1:00 AM isn't that bad. At least I still get a decent night's sleep. But this morning I dragged. Never been much of a morning person.

My husband, on the other hand, is the Energizer Bunny in the morning. So annoying. I drive him nuts at night, reading in bed beside him as he tosses and turns. He drives me nuts in the morning as he rattles off his ideas and the projects he wants to complete for the day. It's as if I have a hangover. Shut up. Be quiet. Stop talking so much and so fast. I'm not awake yet.

***

Doctor's Orders

Yesterday afternoon I saw my psychiatrist at group therapy. After confessing that I've been spending more than ten hours a day (honestly, probably far more) on social media, and that I've been unable to fall asleep at night, my psychiatrist told me that I am socially overstimulating myself. He pointed out that my online activity is a form of social stimulation and reminded me that social stimulation triggers hypomania in me. He also pointed out that I went from no social interaction outside my family in January, to more than ten hours a day in July. So, my dose of Depakote® (divalproex sodium) has been increased by an additional 250 mg a day, and I must limit the hours I spend online, especially at night after dinner.

Dinner serves as an organizing and defining event of the day for me. Family dinner time is almost unplugged; although, honestly, we do allow our son his iPhone on which he watches YouTube videos. We sit in front of the TV as we eat. The three humans in the family enjoy unwinding and passively watching the television as we alternate between watching our son's favorite show, *The Simpsons*, and our shows. Shared favorites include *The Big Bang Theory* and old *Twilight Zone* episodes. Even our huge labradoodle, Thumper, joins in watching. Thumper has been a member of our family since my son was six, which makes him nearly eight-years-old now. For a dog his size, he's well past middle-aged. Our younger, smarter, more rambunctious poodle, Coco, does not find the television nearly as interesting. He's more curious about the physical world around him. Coco has earned the nicknames The Scientist and Quality Control, for he always notices and has to inspect by touching his nose to, and licking anything new or different, as soon as he enters a room.

Okay, so here's my new plan (in addition to more Depakote): dinner, TV, then READ. I'm okay if I use a black background screen with dim grey text while reading in bed beside my sleeping husband. What I must NOT do, because it stimulates me and interferes with my sleep, is switch back and forth to surf the internet to research something that I read, nor can I check on social media and email. I MUST limit social interaction if I am to tamp down this hypomania.

Last night, I must confess (to my husband's gentle dismay and disapproval), after dinner and leisurely watching TV while playing solitaire (relaxing, not stimulating), I did quickly go through my email before heading up to bed. I didn't want to wake up to fifty emails. I already had over twenty. I have reset notifications on my various devices, so that there is no sense of urgency. No more badges telling me how many tweets, Facebook posts, or emails I have. I never allowed those noise-making, obnoxious notifications. The only apps I allow to notify me are cell phone text messages (mostly from my husband and my son and I want to communicate readily with them) and phone calls (again, mostly from family).

Let's see how it goes.

***

Road Trip

We are on our way to Mammoth Mountain, high on the eastern desert side of the Sierras, for a week of downhill mountain biking. I've never had great balance and divalproex sodium (Depakote) makes my inherent klutziness even worse. So, I'll be sticking to beginner slopes. My husband and son, though, will be risking life and limb. They are dare-devils through and through. Besides, they are both quite athletic. My son has always had a gift for balance, physical balance that is. I would not describe any of us as Zenlike. We are a small household of sensitive stimulus-reactive folk, living on a tautly woven web where each of us affects the others.

When my husband and I were first dating, before I had the definitive diagnosis of bipolar disorder, my boss described the two of us as two thoroughbred horses, chomping at the bit, straining to break free of the gate, and start flying down the racetrack. Now we are three racehorses; though, medication slows me down.

***

Crap, I Bent a Bike

Trying to help unload our gear and bags from the car, I moved our minivan closer to our room. Unfortunately, when backing up the minivan, though I did not hear, see, or feel it, my son witnessed me backing up into a concrete piling and in so doing, bending at least one of my husband's bike frames.

Crap. Crap. Crap.

I have a bad history backing up that minivan. Two undeserving, unsuspecting cars have felt the heavy touch of my Toyota Sienna with me at the wheel, obliviously backing out of a parking space. Doesn't take much for a huge old minivan with poor rear window visibility (especially when loaded with a rack of bikes), and a driver with even poorer depth perception to do significant damage.

Shit. Shit. Shit.

The view from our room is beautiful, though.

***

Chair Lifts Freak Me Out

Did I mention that I'm afraid of heights? Not a crippling fear. I do not have acrophobia and do not want to diminish a very real anxiety disorder. Instead I have what I consider a reasonable fear: the fear of falling off high places. Since I have a history of fighting the urge to "fly" off bridges and cliffs, this fear relates to not only a reasonable fear for basic survival, but to a history of manic or hypomanic symptoms. "Stay on the bridge, Kitt, you cannot fly." "Stay on the road, Kitt, you cannot fly. You are not driving *Chitty Chitty Bang Bang*. Luckily, today I only felt the normal level of fear and had no manic desire to fly. Anyway, back to the prosaic...

Mammoth's easiest trail, aside from their skill-building loop, requires taking an open-air chair lift with no safety bar. (Postscript: My husband and son later showed me that there indeed was a safety bar. I didn't see it because it was above my head, and I certainly wasn't looking up any higher. Well, actually, I did enjoy a peak at the summit.) Did I mention that chair lifts freak me out? Well, while my more highly skilled man-boys (husband and teen son) took the gondola high into the clouds, I took the Discovery chair lift alone. So far, twice.

***

Gratitude

Tonight, I am grateful for my son whom I love dearly. To celebrate his fourteenth birthday tomorrow, we are mountain biking on ruggedly beautiful Mammoth Mountain, an ancient volcano lying beside the granite Eastern Sierras of California. As I write, I sit beside my husband, for whom I am very much thankful. I'd find it far more difficult to navigate life without him. Plus, he fathered our son.

Now that I'm blogging, I've befriended many mental health advocates who offer each other, and me, support. For that support and community, I am grateful. Many of the bloggers I've met online, both with and without mental health causes, are incredibly talented writers.

***

Brain Slog Today

Okay, now as the result of overstimulating myself into hypomania and over-work, by obsessively and excessively engaging in social media and spreading myself too thin... I'm totally exhausted, have a headache, and I'm experiencing serious BRAIN SLOG.

That's the only way I can now describe my seeming inability to do what I should be able to do. My brain is on break. It is broke.

***

Exhausted Again

As could be expected, I am exhausted. Have run out of juice. A couple (few?) weeks of hypomania and overstimulation, and now I'm dragging and headachy. Got what I wanted done today. Before I picked up my nephew at the airport late this afternoon, I uploaded a bunch of photos from my iCloud account to Flickr. Added titles to the photos. Need to start adding photos to my blog posts, but I take pictures of flowers, trees, and the sky, not of anything related to my posts. The link to my Flickr account is not working. Got to work on that. In the meantime, goodnight. I'll spend the rest of tonight reading.

The plan this week is modest house painting (very modest expectations of my son and his cousin). I may take them to the pool, to the local beaches, and to the local trails. Friday we'll head on over to my parents' place to visit. They always look forward to visits from their grandsons. My sister and I had sons; I, one, and she, three. Not one daughter.

Until I write again, goodnight and goodbye for now!

***

Sh*t Forgot My Meds Last Night

Last night, amid a change in routine, I forgot to take my night-time medication. When I saw this morning that my pillbox still contained last night's medication, I took a partial night-time dose of divalproex sodium. My current night-time dose is 1000 mg. This morning I took 750 mg; one 500 mg tablet, one 250 mg tablet.

Today I will be sleepy. Crap. I absolutely HATE it when I forget a dose of medication. I feel it immediately. Now I'm very, very tired, since I usually take divalproex before I go to bed, not first thing in the morning. It has sedating side effects. At least I take the extended release version. No doubt, it is time to make some coffee.

***

Thought Wisps

F*ck, what was I thinking? Cannot recall. Had a thought or perhaps even more than one. Something to write for my blog. Now I'm drawing a blank. My mind cannot hold onto thoughts for very long. They slip away. Slip away. Wisps. The thought had to do with removing my MFT license from my description, for I feel out of it. Today in group I felt particularly out of it. Out of practice for so long. Not familiar with the mental health consumers movement, concept of mental health recovery, myriad of psychotherapy treatment modalities, most of which do not fully describe what anyone actually does for most psychotherapists blend theories and practice mocalities, and then do whatever seems to work. In any case, I am not a psychotherapist now. Nor will I be any time soon. Not ready, not as long as my brain fails me so completely.

***

Am I Bipolar or Do I Have Bipolar?

Do I have bipolar disorder or am I bipolar? I know many in the mental health community feel strongly about the meaning of this linguistic distinction. Can I honestly claim that I am not defined by my illness? My brain disorder influences my personality and the way I think. Bipolar disorder defines and limits me in ways I wish it didn't. My mind does not work as well as it once did. I am less intelligent, less productive, and less functional than I once was. The mundane easily overwhelms me. I have an illness that limits me and in doing so, redefines me. I once planned to become a physician but had to let go of that goal and of other goals for I wasn't up to it. I was once an ambitious child, teen, and young woman. Ambition is now beyond me. I mourn the loss of my former self. I mourn the loss of brilliance that was once a part of me.

***

Dual Diagnosis

Twice today peers, both recovering addicts, have suggested that although I do not drink much, I may be an alcoholic because of my relationship with alcohol (and marijuana, for that matter). The statements ring true. Within me lives an alcoholic over whom I must exert tremendous control. I sense a strong genetic and biological predisposition to alcoholism and marijuana abuse. When I was seventeen to thirty, I self-medicated using marijuana to slow my thoughts and make me stupid, offering me relief from my hypo-manic racing thoughts. Still today, when I see or smell alcohol or marijuana, I crave it, and I find myself fighting that craving.

This has been a difficult week for me and my family.

According to the *Journal of the American Medical Association* (November 21, 1990. "Comorbidity of Mental Disorders With Alcohol and Other Drug Abuse." jama.jamanetwork.com/article.aspx?articleid=383975), approximately 50 percent of individuals diagnosed with severe mental illness are affected by substance abuse. About 37 percent of individuals with alcoholism, and 53 percent of individuals with drug addictions have at least one serious mental illness.

***

Manic Temper Tantrum

Last night I blew up and had a full-on manic temper tantrum. I forcefully threw my iPad down and then proceeded to flip over the kitchen table. Crap. I was at the end of my rope. I had overdone it over the weekend, painting the exterior of our house in extreme heat (and too much sun). My husband and I were arguing over home renovations, and I lost it, completely. I hate it when I lose it. At the time, our son was wearing noise cancelling earphones and playing a video game in his room, but he did see me ramping up earlier in the evening, getting increasingly irritable, argumentative, and reactive. I kept telling my husband that I wasn't well, had overdone it, and couldn't deal with discussing the home renovations.

After isolating myself in our bedroom for a while to cool off (and pack an overnight bag, which I did not use), I came back downstairs, and my husband was on the phone with family members trying to find out how his oldest brother was doing. His brother's cancer has rapidly progressed to stage 4. Our 14-year old son came downstairs and tried to lighten the mood by reminding us of family members who successfully fought off cancer, including my mother who faced stage 4 twice and survived. Our teenage son was the voice of reason amidst rage, anxiety, and despair. He shouldn't have to endure my unacceptable behavior, our arguing, or our worries. Prayers are welcome and appreciated.

***

Help, My World is Chaos

We've been in the process of renovating our house over the last three years. My husband and I made the HUGE mistake of buying materials for several major projects up front, making decisions on the spot that should have been deferred and made one project at a time. We ended up with a house and garage filled with materials: cabinetry, paint, flooring, tile. We still have not finished painting the interior walls. Our framed artwork and photos lean up against walls, or lay in piles on tabletops, or in boxes. We had painted most of the downstairs when the interior painting was put on hold so that my husband could install hardwood floors. Then we renovated our bathrooms. Our dry-rotted exterior siding has been replaced. Last Sunday we primed the exterior paint. We also must eventually re-landscape the backyard. Our dogs enjoy the raised open beds too much. Too much fun to dig, bury, and re-dig. We've decided to eventually cede the backyard to our dogs.

Sound overwhelming and chaotic? It is. You should have seen our house when the living room was for months FULL of boxes of oak flooring.

Our dining room table sharing space with bathroom cabinetry. Then, my husband decided to buy a HUGE weight set through Craigslist. Forgive me, I'm venting. The weight set is 8 ft long by 7 ft high by 7 ft wide. It is absolutely ridiculous. My husband and son are NOT serious body builders. My husband was a runner. My son is into downhill mountain bike riding. They are both lean and long-legged. My son insists on working on his bikes in the house. So, I'm embarrassed to have anyone over. EVER. I don't see the point in cleaning because I feel so overwhelmed and buried by the chaos.

***

We Stopped at One Child

When I was pregnant with my son, I was under treatment for depression, but was not yet diagnosed bipolar. That diagnosis I received when he was two. We ended up deciding not to have more children, not because we feared passing on a genetic risk for bipolar disorder, but because one was all we could handle, especially given that our son was EXTREMELY active (later treated for hyperactivity, doing very well now as a teen).

What I did fear, though, was whether I was a good enough mother. I had internalized stigma against the diagnosis of bipolar disorder over that of depression. Internalized stigma is a horrible thing. It eats at your sense of self-worth.

We can be great mothers, whether or not we live with a diagnosis of bipolar disorder. Even if our children *do* inherit the "bipolar gene," treatments are always improving. Think of the improvements over the past 50 years, then project 50 years into the future. Who would be better to obtain treatment and show compassion than a parent who has lived through the same symptoms? But, as my psychiatrist reminds me, we must be careful not to project our symptoms and our fears onto our kids. Just because we have bipolar disorder, does not mean that they will.

***

Excited or Overstimulated?

Volunteer training shadowing an MHA Hearing Advocate last Friday either excited or overstimulated me. There can be a fine line between the two. Since then I've had trouble slowing down and turning off, and found myself glued to laptop, tablet, or iPhone until past my bedtime. I've resorted to taking clonazepam to turn off my brain and fall asleep. Either Saturday or Sunday I slept in past noon. Memory is a bit fuzzy. Do not recall which day. Now, I'm exhausted and in a bit of a slump. I'll recover. Just need to rest up today. Late this afternoon (or what the character Sheldon Cooper of *The Big Bang Theory* coined "pre-evening") I will be attending group therapy. As I was sick last week, my activity with MHA of Orange County as a Hearing Advocate trainee will be news!

***

Time to Crawl under the Covers

This time of year can be difficult for those of us with mood disorders. The recent time change made what the clock says is the late afternoon now the dark of night. My dogs know it is the night-time. They are not fooled by our clocks. Seasonal affective disorder now kicks in. Our bodies are affected by fewer hours of sun, overcast skies, and colder temperatures. As the outside temperatures cool, we just want to cocoon and crawl back under the covers. Granted, it is not so cool here in southern California, but even going from the 90s to the 60s has a significant effect on mood.

***

Holiday Drinking Triggers Me

Holidays I find unsettling. Not only are the days far too short, but visiting family can destabilize me and trigger bipolar symptoms. I acutely feel a genetic predisposition to alcoholism, drinking minimally, but craving intoxication, more so when triggered. The holidays trigger me for I am surrounded by family members who drink, some who drink to excess daily.

It pains me to see those I love dearly drinking or, worse-yet, drunk. What pains me the most is seeing my once vibrant father suffering from alcohol-related dementia. His cognitive abilities deteriorate quickly throughout the day and evening as he gets progressively more intoxicated. Both my mother and I become more emotional labile, sensitive, and reactive as we drink. Such is a recipe for repeated family drama.

Still, I desire the intoxicating effect of alcohol. When watching TV, I track alcoholic beverages. In *The Big Bang Theory*, they hold and gulp wine in every episode. In *Blue Bloods*, Tom Selleck drinks whiskey. When grocery shopping, I am very aware of the aisle with alcohol and try to avoid it. Unfortunately, the wines face those snacks my husband and son enjoy.

When I socialize with people who are drinking, I crave alcohol, and I, too, drink. I do not drink to excess, but I drink for a biochemical reaction, for my brain to be slowed down and numbed, for that feeling of intoxication, not because I enjoy the flavor. I am no connoisseur. I am, perhaps, an alcoholic who drinks minimally. Likewise, I still remember what marijuana smells like. I still have a visceral reaction when remembering that heady scent, when recounting how I used marijuana decades ago for relief, to slow down and be stupid.

***

Ambivalent about My Dogs

Although I love my dogs, I am still suffering from PTSD from an incident in which I could not control them, and they viciously attacked a greyhound who had just been attacked by another standard poodle the previous week. I took full responsibility for the attack and paid the poor dog's veterinary bill. Still, I fear walking Thumper. He's too big and I cannot control him.

Interesting metaphor just occurred to me, piggybacking an interpretation offered by my psychologist Friday when I described my fear of violent and agitated men (specifically, agitated and violent, seriously mentally ill men). She asked if I may fear that part of me that rages, that goes to that red zone where my rational mind cannot control my behavior. Yes. Yes, I do fear that part of me, and regret the damage done to those I love when I rage.

***

Dear Younger Me

You fuel your rage by seeing a psychoanalyst one to three times a week, exploring over and over how you had been abused as a child. You deepen your depression by studying psychodynamic theory in graduate school. Doing so defeats you and undermines your mental health. Yes, therapy will enable you to work through issues you have with your parents, but what is left unsaid is the fact that your parents love you.

Of course they are not perfect. Nobody is perfect. We are all "dysfunctional" to some extent or another. Yes, it is difficult to grow up in an alcoholic household, but your family loves YOU. Believe me, loving you is quite difficult.

Do not defensively rage against your father when he suggests that "Wouldn't it be great if you could just take a pill and feel better?" He was right. He merely suggested a medical solution to your long-standing struggle with depression, and you jumped all over him.

Your bipolar disorder, what was then diagnosed as depression and interpreted as aggression turned inward against yourself, is not caused by abusive parenting. You have a biological disorder of the brain. You did yourself no favors by smoking pot from seventeen years old to the time you completely came undone at thirty. You did yourself no favors by taking shrooms, dropping acid, or, on one particularly stupid occasion, snorting cocaine. You did yourself no favors by drinking alcohol. You damaged your fragile brain. You may very well have tipped the balance.

Your childhood was not perfect. No one's is. Your parents have had their own struggles. Now you know, mood disorders are genetic and often self-medicated with alcohol. Working with families as a therapist, you learned compassion for your parents. You saw the love these parents had for their children as they struggled to parent them. You shook your head when staff vilified adoptive parents of children with severe mental health and behavioral issues. You knew it was not the adoptive parents' fault that their children had brain disorders, in utero exposure to alcohol and drugs, or extreme child abuse and neglect by others. Still, clinical staff judged the desperate adoptive parents, rather than show compassion and offer support.

Kitt, if only you had used your Kaiser insurance for mental health treatment, rather than pay out-of-pocket to see an analyst. If only you had seen a psychiatrist at a younger age, your life would have been different. You would have properly cared for your fragile brain earlier in your life. Your loved ones would have been spared your rages and mood swings. Perhaps. Perhaps, to some extent. Then again, perhaps not.

I cannot change the past. I can only move forward from here. I must forgive the Kitt who blamed her parents, rather than see a medical doctor. To all the many therapists who saw me, and never recommended that I see a psychiatrist, what were you thinking? They, too, I must forgive, for I did not "look bipolar" as I've been told on more than one occasion. My worst behavior is reserved for those I love the most.

Kitt, forgive me for not being proactive, for not taking care of your brain, for blaming others for something over which they had little to no control.

***

Life Simplified

There are a seemingly infinite number of excellent blogs to follow, read, like, and comment on. There are only 24 hours in a day, and I'm running out of steam. My New Year Resolution is to protect my time and energy. I am doing so now.

Now I free my time for writing original content and for living my life unplugged. I have books to read and training to attend. Starting January 31st, I will attend my local NAMI Orange County chapter Provider Education Program, with the hope of becoming a Provider Educator.

We must get our reactive dogs into dog training; actually, the humans in the family need training on how to communicate with our dogs.

Our house is a mess. Clutter surrounds us on every horizontal surface. I'm not the best housekeeper in the world, not that I ever aspired to be such. Still, I should clean the house every now and again. No doubt I should cook more often, for when I do, we eat healthier. (The "shoulds" are adding up here.) Luckily, we have options for healthy take-out nearby. We can get sushi, Persian salmon kabobs, grilled or ceviche fish tacos, and Indian food within a few miles. Not bad at all.

Did I mention that we must finish painting the interior and exterior of our house and possibly heighten our fences to reduce stimulation of our territorial dogs? Oh, and I'm married to a civil engineer. Translation: he's a consummate do-it-yourselfer. He's handy and has accomplished a lot, including installing solid oak floors, but there is still much to be done.

To top it all off, extended family members we love dearly fight cancer and multiple sclerosis. Oh, and just in case you didn't read my tag line, I have bipolar disorder, and I'm a mom. No wonder I feel overwhelmed.

***

Crashing Down

I often feel like I have fallen down from up high and am less of a person than I once was. But I was not a star fixed in the sky; instead, I shot high, quickly achieving goals by working extremely long hours at high intensity, then would come crashing down. Over and over.

***

Refresh, Energize, and Rejuvenate

The last experience I had that left me feeling refreshed, energized, and rejuvenated was the last time I took a bath. Yes, it's that simple. A bath. Enveloped by warm water. Warmth that may well be therapeutic, may alleviate feelings of social isolation.

Walks in which I notice natural beauty – the beauty of a flower, tree branches, or the sky – also leave me feeling refreshed, energized, rejuvenated, and connected to something greater than myself -nature.

What strikes me is that both are easy to do, yet I do not do them regularly. Bathe: feel refreshed, energized, rejuvenated, and less alone. Walk: feel refreshed, energized, and rejuvenated, and quite literally, grounded.

The question in mind is, when did I last do so? Did I take a warm bath yesterday? The day before? I do not recall. The last time I took a walk? I know that I did so over the holidays. Since then I've struggled with lingering stomach flu symptoms. Still, I could take a short walk. Look at the sky. Enjoy the beauty of a flower. Not to mention, spend some quality time with my husband who, with our two dogs, eagerly awaits me to join him on a walk.

Perhaps today I will do both, walk *and* bathe. Now that's an accomplish-ment.

UFDATE: Walk with husband, but no dogs: check (even took some photo-graphs). Warm bath: check. Refreshed, energized, and rejuvenated: check, check, and check.

***

Mental Illness, Religion, and Spirituality

Healing, recovery, or simply living with a serious mental illness such as bipolar disorder may require medical, psychological, and spiritual support. Struggling with mental illness can at times *feel* like spiritual war. As some-one living with bipolar disorder, while in the deepest of depressions, I've experienced what I can only describe as a living Hell, and while hypomanic or manic, I've believed myself called by God to a higher purpose.

When churches demonize or ostracize the mentally ill, they quite frankly sin by hurting those in need of love and compassion. Many people first go to their faith community for help. Churches and faith communities MUST be compassionate and refer people to the proper resources to address their psychiatric or psychological needs. Belief and prayer do not make brain disorders miraculously disappear, but a loving community (religious or secular) can offer support, encouragement, and hope.

***

I, Too, Am Not Okay

I, too, am not okay, and I'm okay with it. Often other people do not understand what they cannot see. For many years I wondered, do other people think like this? Do other people have to tell themselves not to drive off that cliff, not to push that stranger in front of the BART train, not to hang up the telephone in mid-conversation for no reason whatsoever? I used to think, if so, then why aren't more people driving off cliffs, pushing people in front of subway trains, and rudely hanging up the phone mid-sentence? They are not doing these things, yet I have to tell myself over and over not to do it. For years I struggled with manic symptoms, intrusive thoughts and disturbing impulses, without knowing what they were. Without realizing that I had a treatable mental illness. I knew I was depressed. I mean, wanting to kill yourself is clearly a symptom of depression. That I got. The other stuff, not so much.

***

Fried – Just Fried

Today I went to a writers' group, and now I am just wiped out. Social stimulation exhausts me. I had a great time, but I'm just not up for it. Just not up for two hours of conversation. Damn fucking brain disorder. I HATE bipolar disorder. My brain is FRIED.

***

Impulsive Much?

Yes, I'm impulsive. I get so excited; I cannot contain it.

Okay, here's the thing: I get stimulated in social situations. Too stimulated. Too excited. Too impulsive. I take over. Hog the floor. Talk too much. Not so good at sharing. So, can I really participate in give-and-take social situations? Can I be a member of a presentation panel and wait my turn? Can I give a presentation and then share the floor? Can I hold myself back? Can I hold my tongue? Can I limit myself? Can I do that? Honestly, I do not know if I can. It goes against my nature, or is it my illness, my symptoms? Hypomanic much? Impulsive much? Poor boundaries much? Poor social skills much? Crap.

***

Ten Year Anniversary of Hospitalization

Ten years ago, two weeks preceding and including Valentine's Day, I was hospitalized. Twenty years ago, I experienced a psychotic break during the same season: this season, the season of Lent. Though I do not attend church, this season moves me deeply. I could write more about seasonal affective disorder and how those of us with bipolar disorder predictably cycle during different seasons. But, for today, Valentine's Day, I will enjoy the evening with my husband. Thank God I am not in the hospital this Valentine's Day. Thank God I can enjoy the occasion at home with my husband and son.

***

Bipolar Disorder and Seasonal Affective Disorder

Spring has Sprung, and the Birds are Busy

Outside a cacophony of birds loudly pronounce that they have important work to do, nests to build, eggs to lay, offspring to bring into the world. Spring has sprung. The sun is bright. The season of rebirth is here. Hypomania is officially here, as well, folks. Yes, I have concurrent bipolar disorder and seasonal affective disorder. In spring, I ramp. Ramp I do indeed. Perhaps it›s a good time to visit my psychiatrist. Perhaps I do not need to take an antidepressant on top of my mood stabilizer now.

Near midnight, I resort to taking clonazepam to fall asleep. In fact, just one dose won't do it at times like this. I lie in bed, then take a second pill, the bottle of which I keep bedside for just this purpose. I even chew the pills so that I don't have to wait for my stomach to digest them. I want sleep. I need sleep. I beg the mucus membranes in my mouth to quickly absorb the medication into my bloodstream. Then, I lie in bed some more, mind hyper-alert, body fatigued, and finally go to the medicine cabinet to add melatonin and antihistamines to the mix, hoping that now I can somehow turn off that brain and rest. Past midnight, my mind is wide awake, thirsting to get back online and work, which does not help, not at all.

To top things off, tomorrow – Tuesday morning – I have a Social Security Disability Mental Status Exam. Oh, joy. Yes, I am anxious. Crap. Very anxious.

Worst of all, and perhaps what I should have led with, one of my brothers-in-law is fighting for his life, and perhaps losing the battle against lung cancer He is still in his fifties. He is one of my husband's two older fraternal twin brothers, both once Marines. My husband has always looked up to his older brothers and turned to them for advice on how to fix things. They looked out for him when he was a kid. My heart goes out to my husband, who is in great pain. Someone he loves dearly is dying, will be entering hospice care soon, and he can do nothing to fix it, to make his brother's pain and cancer go away. I can do nothing to fix it. All we can do is love, pray, and reach out to share that love and those prayers.

September 2013, I started writing this blog when my father in law was hospitalized for sepsis. We almost lost him, but he is still with us today, thank God. Crisis, my inability to do anything to help with the crisis – aside from loving my husband and praying – triggered my hypomania then.

***

Childhood Trauma of Parental Mental Illness

At the beginning of this week, a woman who had been horrifically abused by a mother diagnosed with manic depressive psychosis read my poem "Suicide Infanticide" and was understandably enraged. My poem described a fleeting and deeply disturbing psychotic thought I had postpartum. Her comment deeply troubled me and made me question my adequacy as a mother. I responded to her comment, later removed the entire comment thread, and finally late Thursday afternoon as I revised this post, restored the comments.

Early drafts of this post included an edited version of her comment in which I removed her references to parenticide-suicide, for she directed them at me and my child. But this post is about compassion, and my poem was about "Suicide Infanticide" after all, so why shouldn't I welcome her to express her pain, rage, and indignation in her words.

Compassion requires me to listen to and understand her point of view, take my ego out of the equation, and not see her words as an attack on me as an individual, but on me as someone who represents her abusive homicidal mother and a mental health advocacy movement that she believes does not represent or protect the children of mentally ill parents. The life she describes is horrific. Not all children of mentally ill parents live horrific lives, but parental mental illness is a real-life stressor on children and can have lasting negative health consequences.

One reason I wrote «Suicide Infanticide» and «Bad Mom» – aside from the poems forcing themselves out of me to voice disturbing thoughts I had kept secret – is that I wanted to address exactly these issues. There are real consequences to mental illness when it is not adequately treated or when it does not respond to treatment. I own the effects that I have on those I love.

Those of us who live with mental illness owe it to our children to maintain our own mental health. We owe it to our children to not act out our symptoms. We owe it to our children to not burden them with our illness. We owe it to our children to be the best parents we can be, to be what Donald Winnicott coined a «good enough parent.»

***

Spring is REALLY LOUD

Springtime can trigger seasonal affective disorder (SAD) in those with depression and bipolar disorder. For those of us with bipolar disorder, SAD can trigger mania and hypomania. The stressors of these changes contributed to my psychiatric hospitalization a decade ago.

As spring has approached and the days have lengthened, I have had mild symptoms of hypomania, including insomnia, which I addressed with my psychiatrist by reducing my SSRI dose. We left my dosage of divalproex sodium (Depakote) the same. Initially, we tried halving my dose of the SSRI escitalopram (Lexapro) to 2.5 mg for six days, with the intent of removing the SSRI altogether. But I found myself unable to stay awake during the daytime, so I remain on 5 mg.

To me, spring is a cacophony of noises accompanying the frenzy of renewed life. The days are longer. The birds build nests and make it known loudly and clearly with their calls that they are mating and starting anew. All that springtime bursting and bustling of new life, is stimulating, and for me, overstimulating.

***

Passed My SSDI Review (Whew!)

Spring triggers hypomania and agitation in me. As many of my readers already know, one spring more than twenty years ago, tricyclic antidepressant misuse, seasonal affective disorder, and underlying undiagnosed bipolar disorder resulted in a week-long manic psychotic break.

Today, I update you on my recent Social Security Disability Income (SSDI) eligibility review. When I went in for my recent SSDI review interview, it benefited me that I was hypomanic and agitated since spring was approaching and I had not yet seen my psychiatrist to adjust my medications.

Just one look at the form they had me fill out was enough to know that my mind was all over the place. I had multiple arrows leading to notes in the margins of the form to give more detailed answers to the form's supposedly simple questions. I was unable to contain myself to the form. Similarly, when answering the psychiatrist's questions, I was all over the place with my answers. She had to stop me several times to get me to focus, to contain me. Succinct, I was NOT. Anyway, at the end of the interview the very nice psychiatrist told me I gave her WAY MORE than she needed, but within all that I said, she got what she needed. She asked me how I would describe myself at the time, and I answered "agitated." She nodded. Yep, I was agitated.

The review determined that I am still eligible for benefits. Yay! Don't have to go out and start cycling (as in mood cycling, not bicycling) as I look for work.

The week following the SSDI interview, I saw my psychiatrist to reduce my dose of SSRI antidepressant (of which I already took a very low dose). We planned on weaning me from it completely, but in doing so, I started to become depressed, so we kept it at half my previous dose.

***

Holy Friday

For those who do not believe in the value of religious mythology, I do. Whether or not the stories happened, whether or not they are literally true, they offer messages that are true. The meaning, the message, is what moves me.

In Christianity, today is Good Friday or Holy Friday. Holy Friday commemorates the crucifixion of Jesus Christ and his death at Calvary. The message I take away from Holy Friday is that God knows our pain, for Jesus, as God incarnate, suffered. I take this story to heart, for it has helped me to realize that I am NOT alone in my suffering. God knows, loves and forgives me.

Depressed I believed that I was alone, unloved, unforgivably flawed, and not worthy of life. I believed that the world would be a better place without me in it. I expected perfection from myself and had trouble accepting my brokenness. I hid my pain. I hid in shame. I had no compassion and no forgiveness for myself. If an omnipotent being can take human form and suffer pain on my behalf (on ALL our behalf), then I can forgive and love myself, I can feel compassion for myself, I can accept myself. I am not alone in my suffering. None of us is.

You are loved. You are not alone. Love yourself. You are worthy of your own love. Have compassion for yourself. Forgive yourself your brokenness. It is okay to not be okay. Take care.

***

What Happens? Hypomania Happens

What happens when I over-involve myself in social media? I'm all over the place and overactive. What happens when I engage in a protracted blog comment debate over my involvement with NAMI, typing away into the wee hours of the morning and continuing over subsequent days?

What happens when I participate in the Semicolon Project's Facebook event "to raise public awareness against Depression, Anxiety, Self-harm and Suicide," and feel drawn to reach out to as many people as possible, but my arms, my heart, my fingers, and my keyboard only reach so far?

What happens when I involve myself in *Tha.Speakeasy* – an awesome and/ but stimulating Facebook spoken word event Friday and Saturday – hosted by the incomparable T.A. (Tamara) Woods?

What happens when I realize that in my focus on bipolar blogs, I have neglected reading and listening to so many fabulous works of writing, of poetry, of spoken word, of music, and then desperately try to play catch-up? (One of my Twitter followers thought that I'd been hacked for I tweeted out so much content.)

All this after a very busy weekend. I had spent a day and evening with others, people besides my husband and son. I went to a NAMI Advocacy training Friday, April 10th. That night I inadvertently crashed a dinner party hosted by the Executive Director and President of my local NAMI. Oops

The next day I drove an hour to and an hour from my parents' home to do their income taxes; the day after that I finished our taxes.

Finally, on Monday I managed to get my son to school after his week-long spr ng break, only to be called to pick him up from the nurse's office two hours into his school day. So, amid this all, my son has either been home on vacation, or home sick with gastroenteritis.

What Happens? Hypomania Happens

***

Thoughts Intrude

Leave Me Alone

Thoughts intrude

Throw plate in sink

Let it shatter loudly

I see myself doing it

The image, the impulse, are there

There - in my mind

No I respond

Turn left NOW in front of oncoming traffic

No No! No! Don't do it

Wait for the green arrow

Yell at, argue with, my son, my husband

Pick a fight with them

No! Do not do it

Must fight the thoughts

Must fight the impulses

They make no sense

I'm irritable

In a mixed state

Somewhat hypomanic

Not suicidal

There is no intent behind them

Just intrusive thoughts

Unwelcome images and impulses

Without reason

Without cause

Except this pain

These insistent hormones

Nasty cramps

Super irritable

Why?

It's been months

I think

Since last I bled

I'm 51, 52 this August

Give it up already

Stop menstruating

It's not going to happen

No more babies

From this empty fibrous womb

So, stop it

Leave me alone

Leave my body alone

Stop with the pain

Stop behaving

Like a fertile woman

I AM OLD

LEAVE ME BE

Let me become

The crone, the hag

I've earned it

Leave me be

Let me rest

Enough

***

Perimenopausal Woman

Sick of being irritable. Sick of having to warn my husband that I'm in a bad mood. Ready for menopause. Ready for this interminable period of transit on to end.

Perimenopause and menopause complicate living with bipolar disorder, depression, or anxiety. Hormonal changes affect mental health. According to WebMD ("The Emotional Roller Coaster of Menopause." Retrieved May 30, 2019 at https://www.webmd.com/menopause/guide/emotional-roller-coaster), as estrogen levels drop before menopause, women can experience the following emotional changes: irritability, feelings of sadness, lack of motivation, anxiety, aggressiveness, difficulty concentrating, fatigue, mood changes, and tension.

The poem "Emotions Fragile" offers a taste of how I felt when perimenopausal. Now I'm happily post-menopause and more stable. Having my hormones level is a game-changer.

Emotions Fragile

Hot flashes

Warm flashes

Tears held inside

Emotions fragile

Menopause is a bitch

But this bitch can handle it

If I can ride the ups and downs of bipolar

I can ride this one out

***

Yesterday Was a Bust

Feeling Blue like a Failure

Yesterday, I blew it. First, I had vertigo in the morning. The night before my son had complained of getting dizzy walking up the stairs and collapsed into bed. Monday morning, I had to hold onto walls to keep my balance.

Using the vertigo as an excuse (probably a good reason to avoid driving, though I did take my kid to and from school), I bailed attending an Orange County Community Action Advisory Committee meeting. Why I even went to the previous month's meeting, I do not know. I don't even use any county services. I suppose I could. I am on disability. There are services available, as well as nonprofit peer support groups nearby. But, I don't.

Eventually I bail on every group (but I am still married, and no matter how much of a failure I feel as a mother, I haven't run away). Honestly, I just do not feel comfortable with the whole group membership thing, and so I shirk all expectations. I've trained to be a NAMI volunteer, but I've done minimal, absolutely minimal volunteering. I'm a farce. A joke. An illusion. I feel like a total fucking failure.

I even bailed on going out for our anniversary dinner, which suited my husband. He'd just as soon put his jammies on after work. But I was isolating myself and neglecting putting myself together, making myself look and feel pretty, or at least presentable. I want to be waited on hand and foot, I wanted to eat delicious food, I just wasn't up for going out to a restaurant. I wasn't up for going OUT, period. I failed once again as a mother, losing it when my son threw a fit. I responded with a fit of my own. Fuck. Fuck. Fuck. I JUST CANNOT HOLD IT TOGETHER ANYMORE. I'm undone. I'm completely undone.

Now, I'm debating bailing on meeting an acquaintance for lunch. She's a lovely woman writer, a mother (no doubt a better mother), who is a member of OC Writers, a local writers' group which I have not gone to in quite some time. Shit.

***

Time to Find a New Therapist

Time for a change. When I last saw my psychologist, she equated allowing my son to play video games to allowing him to smoke marijuana. She said that the two did the same neurological and psychological damage, that video games produce emotional cripples unable to make intimate relationships. She was quite incensed about it.

I do not need that kind of reaction. I need a more balanced approach. I'm parenting a teen boy, and I need help in doing so. Teen boys play video games. I'm not going to cut my son off from his friends, but, somehow, we must do a better job of setting limits.

Here's the difficulty: I have seen this psychologist on and off for ten years. We moved away twice during that time -- once to Eugene and once to the Mojave Desert -- and returned to south Orange County after both moves.

Anyway, tomorrow we are seeing the psychologist who collaborates with my psychiatrist for help with our (my) relationship with our son. I may enlist him as my psychologist. We'll see how it goes.

***

Sometimes Taking a Bath is an Achievement

Sometimes simply taking a bath is a major achievement. Not quite sure when I last bathed or showered. Friday, perhaps? I really can't recall.

Yesterday I actually exercised. Yes, that's right, I exercised. Worked out with weights, used a treadmill for a couple of minutes (very little), and used an elliptical for several minutes. Not a huge workout, not enough to work up a sweat. But today I can feel it in my glutes and pecs. (Don't I sound like a gym rat? I just call them my ass and chest.)

Anyway, this morning, after taking my son to the school, handling email and updating social media, I took a bath. Then I managed to go grocery shopping. In the afternoon, I took my son to his allergist for an immuno-logical work-up. We have a lab requisition for a long list of tests. Once the lab results are complete, we'll return to the allergist to see the results and take the next step. Got to get my boy healthier so he doesn't miss as much school next year.

By the way, I'm absolutely exhausted. Just spent.

***

Simple Self Care

Got my hair cut today - a simple act of self-care. Took a picture of it, but didn't like the photo. Hate how I look in photos. Same haircut as last time, but maintaining the cut helps me to feel better about myself. Plus, it feels quite luxurious to have someone wash, blow dry, cut, and comb my hair. Heck, I don't even blow dry my hair. Sometimes I don't even brush it.

***

Blocked, But Why?

I no longer notice when or if I'm blocked or unfriended on social media. Perhaps I no longer inundate others with content (perhaps I still do. It's subjective). As I'm not as active online and as my focus is not just on myself, I've gained some new readers and lost others.

Yesterday I found that someone blocked me on Twitter, and I didn't know why. It hurt and reminded me of someone else blocking me on Twitter, and of yet another person who unfriended me on Facebook and informed me that she had done so (why, I have no idea, she didn't say). The bottom line is: My feelings are hurt. I wonder what I did wrong. I wonder if I did something to injure the other person. I know I post A LOT. Profuse posting can overwhelm others, burying them under a barrage of tweets, posts, and links to follow. I am bipolar after all, so my hypomanic activity is partly symptomatic. I'm passionate, as well, and feel compelled to share great content over social media. In addition, I realize that medication and psychotherapy has helped me, so that someone medication-resistant may not find me a helpful support. Still, it hurts.

***

Burns

As bipolar disorder is a spectrum disorder, I know that my symptoms are less severe than others. That's not to say that I do not cycle or that I'm asymptomatic.

I've screamed at and hit my son. I've flipped the kitchen table and slammed doors. I've been psychotic and struggled with intrusive thoughts and impulses. I've also rapidly cycled and had mixed episodes. These symptoms, and the fact that I was psychiatrically hospitalized, qualify me for a diagnosis of bipolar type I. I usually do not state which "type" of bipolar disorder I have, for my mental illness is somewhat fluid. Sometimes I'm more stable than other times.

Bipolar disorder is a spectrum disorder. Some of us have it easier than others. That is why I was not diagnosed as bipolar for decades. Hypomania looks much different than full-blown mania. Much. Mania can be incredibly destructive. Hypomania (aside from the irritable bitchiness and rage) can result in overachievement and make one look more like a superstar than someone struggling with mental illness. In fact, my workaholism IS a symptom, but a very different symptom than others.

Some people's depression and bipolar disorder does NOT respond to treatment, to medication, to ECT (electroconvulsive therapy), to CBT (cognitive behavioral therapy), to mindfulness, to any medical, psychotherapeutic, nutritional or alternative treatment, and it is NOT their fault.

It is WRONG for us to deny each other, to put each other down, to expect life to be positive all the time. In fact, there is no positive without negative. There is no light without the dark. Reality is complex.

***

Now that I'm Home Typing

One step at a time. Get out more. Socialize more. Isolate less. Do more. Sit less. Read a good novel.

Now that I'm at home typing, I realize that I want to write more and read fewer blogs. My mental health requires that I stop overextending myself on social media. I want to use it as a useful tool without feeling obligated to read and share so much content. I simply CANNOT continue at this pace for so many hours a day. I absolutely must write more and read less.

Honestly, I'm at the point where reading autobiographical material detailing bipolar symptoms triggers me. In doing so, I re-experience my highs, my lows, my psychosis, my mixed states, my rapid cycling. I must be more judicious in my choice of reading material. I need an escape from bipolar disorder. I may have to severely curtail my reading of other mental health blogs, and instead enjoy some good novels.

I still want to share great content. I still want to maintain my online friendships. I'm honored to be part of such a mutually supportive online community. I hope that I will not lose my cyber friends by not reading and commenting on their work. Unfortunately, that's a risk I take in curtailing my reading and commenting.

So many bloggers produce so much great work. I'm just blown away by how many talented writers are out there telling their stories. But I need to step forward, to move on. Not to stop blogging, for I enjoy doing so. Not to stop sharing great information. Not to stop supporting others. But to curtail my reading of potentially triggering material. To move past focusing on bipolar disorder and mental illness. To allow my mind a rest. To allow my mind to travel to fictional, fantastical places where it has NOT been. To feel free.

One step at a time. Get out more. Socialize more. Isolate less. Do more. Sit less. Read a good novel.

Sounds like a plan to me.

***

Taking a Break

Putting on the brakes and taking a brief break from social media. Limiting triggers to ramping hypomania by trying to unplug until next week. I will catch up on comments next week.

Have a full social calendar over the next few days. Tonight, out with a couple of friends to the Improv in Irvine. Tomorrow and Friday volunteering at NAMI Orange County. Saturday is my husband's company picnic.

WAY more than I usually can take on. I may have to bail on something. If so, that's okay.

My readers and my therapist helped me make this decision. Thanks!

***

Who Am I Really?

Who am I really?

Mystic bipolar

Crazy bitch

Compassionate healer

Mental health advocate

Creative, passionate, intelligent

Wife and mother

Living purposefully

That purpose unfolds daily

As I parent my son

As I write, as I blog

As I connect with others

As I share mental health resources

As I dip my toe into volunteer work

Honestly, though, I'm a diva

Who belongs on stage

Preaching her message

For all to hear

***

Words Fly

I remember when I couldn't hold the letters of a word together long enough to make sense of them. They flew off in all directions or got all jumbled. I simply could not read no matter how hard I tried. Even if I forced myself to concentrate, to focus, to glue one letter to the next until I could put them together to form a word and then to make sense of that one word, its meaning was lost before I got on to the next. The letters would not hold together to form words, the words would not hold together to form sentences. Their meaning was completely lost on me. That is the brain FUCKED UP royally. No doubt about it.

***

Slowed Down My Mind

I feel guilty that I cannot perform.

Okay, so here's what I did last week. My son and I got sick with the flu. The flu forced me to stop, to hesitate, to slow down my ramping hypomania. Instead of volunteering my time at NAMI and getting overstimulated by doing so, the flu forced me to stay at home.

Honestly, I believe it just may be where I belong. I can handle small amounts of social interaction, but my mind starts spinning when I'm exposed to others' needs. I start offering to fix everything. I overextend myself. I overwork.

Before my hospitalization a decade ago, I was a major workaholic. I seem unable to work for or with others without overextending myself, without depleting myself.

I Give Up (Again)

I Admit Defeat. I Surrender. I Let Go.

Here is where I must admit defeat or acknowledge my limitations and sensitivity to social stimulation. I've been hypomanic since I began coming into the NAMI Orange County office to volunteer, and since I offered to help with social media. Apparently, both overstimulate me. I love everyone at the NAMI office and so want to help, but I must acknowledge my own limitations and slow down.

I still very much look forward to participating in my local NAMIWalks, and raising as much money as possible. I still very much look forward to becoming an Ending the Silence presenter in local high schools and a Provider Education panelist.

Of course, I will continue to shout out for NAMI and good mental health as myself and as a NAMI volunteer.

Sorry to my friends at the NAMI Orange County office. I always do this: take something on that I cannot handle and then back off.

In one of the coloring books my sister gave me for my birthday to help me with my ramping hypomania, I found this apt quote:

> Letting go helps us to live in a more peaceful state of mind and
> helps restore our balance. It allows others to be responsible for

themselves and for us to take our hands off situations that do not belong to us. This frees us from unnecessary stress.

- Melody Bettie

My problem is that I want to help everyone, rescue all, offer of myself what I really cannot spare.

***

I Don't Want to Write About Suicide

I don't want to write about suicide

I don't want the image of her

Clinging onto a chain link fence

Chef's knife in hand

Chef's knife inside of her

Looking through the chain link

At kids playing in the park

She mourned the loss of her son

She could not contain her grief

She could not hold on

She had other children

They no longer had a mother

My father no longer had a cousin

I no longer had a cousin once removed

When I was eighteen

I, too, wanted to kill myself

I thought the world

Better off without me

My family

Better off without me

The emotional pain

Unbearable

A living Hell

But I didn't kill myself

I sought help

I got help

But I was not a mother

Grieving the loss of her son

***

Maybe I'm Just a Loner

The world needs loners, too.

What's so bad about being a loner? Why is "social isolation" always referred to negatively? Can't individuals have different needs? Some of us cannot tolerate social stimulation. Some of us do better alone, with a small family, with a close partner. Some of us do not do well in groups.

***

Lost in the Crowd

Lost in the crowd

Out of my natural surroundings

Out of my home

Out of my neighborhood

At a busy cafe

Surrounded by businesspeople

On their lunch break

I'm unmoored

Uncertain of conventions

Where do I order my food?

Do I pay first?

Where do I stand to wait?

So many people

What should I do?

Overwhelmed

Feel out of it

Freaking out inside

Looking okay on the outside

Maybe – maybe not

Inside screaming

LET ME OUT OF HERE

Too loud

Too chaotic

Too crowded

Wish I had indulged

Gone to the hotel restaurant

Been waited on

Finally, I got my food

Sat in the corner

In the spot I had scoped out

Music and voices clamor

Still, as I sit and eat, I shake

Pick at my salad

Then rush back out

To fresh air and open space

***

Art Tames Racing Thoughts

I find creating art and writing a good release for racing thoughts. Coloring, especially, helps to slow down my thoughts and quell anxiety.

When I go on walks, I like to take photos of nature, especially flowers and cloudscapes. The photos I've taken over the last two years. Walking outside in nature and taking the time to appreciate beauty helps me with my moods. At the same time, I must be sure to not overexpose myself to the sun, for it triggers hypomania. The monoprints I created almost two decades ago when I lived with a diagnosis of dysthymia, well before I was diagnosed bipolar. The doodles I've done recently, as I've found coloring and doodling helpful in grounding me, in slowing down racing thoughts and overcoming anxiety.

I am not creative despite or because of my mental illness. I simply am creative. Even when medicated properly and asymptomatic, I am creative. Medication does not turn my creativity off. Using creativity can help me to manage my symptoms, it can be a release, but it is not dependent on me having a diagnosable mental illness. What I want to get across is the importance of self-care, including medication, if needed, and psychother-apy. Art, photography and writing do not take the place of medication or psychotherapy, they are adjuncts to traditional treatment modalities.

***

Fingers Move as Mind Races

Fingers need to move

Nervous hypomanic energy

prompts them to keep busy

Just as my thoughts

my mind

will not be silent

will not slow down

will not rest

My fingers, too, will not be still

so I play Solitaire

or now type

as an outlet

for hypomanic agitation

***

Medication Mishaps

Hypomanic to Exhausted

This week I've been completely exhausted. Twice I forgot to take my mood stabilizer at night. The first time, I didn't realize it until late the next afternoon - too late to take my missed dose. The next time I realized it the following morning and immediately took the previous night's dose.

I became hypomanic due to the first error, publishing three (or more?) posts on Sunday. The second mishap compounds the first and explains why I feel like I'm dragging myself through molasses this week.

Although I'm physically exhausted, I cannot fall asleep without taking sleep meds, resorting to twice my prescribed dose (which my psychiatrist okayed in the past; it's still a reasonable dose). When I'm stable, I do not have to take meds to fall asleep.

Oh, and Friday my husband and I attended our next-door neighbors' daughter's quinceañera, which was lovely, but probably threw me off. Social stimulation triggers my mood cycling.

***

Broken Brain

Brain broken

Frustrating

Do not remember

Must constantly relearn

Brain not functioning properly

Not functioning as it once did

Must constantly relearn

Damn, I hate bipolar disorder

***

Worn Out

Exhausted

Overwhelmed

Not thinking clearly

Not able to complete sentences

Not able to answer direct questions

Fumbling with language

With spoken language

With what I hear

With what I read

So sleepy

Feared falling asleep

Driving to doctor's office

Door locked

Looked at calendar

Over an hour early

Went back to parked car

Overlooking hill of eucalyptus

Enjoyed view

Tolerated gardeners

Noisy leaf blowers

Those things should be illegal

Wish I had slept

That extra hour

Though not sure

It would have helped

Seems there's no refilling

This empty tank

No overcoming

This fatigue right now

Seasonal and situational

Wait it out?

Perhaps

Not sure

***

Day Tripper

I am a day tripper.

I space out when driving.

Overshoot where I'm going.

All the sudden come out of

my daydream and have no idea...

Oh, crap! I missed my turn.

I've done it for long distances in the past.

I'm just a little bit of a space cadet, and

you know, apparently

I, like, gesture and

make expressions and

talk to myself

when I'm doing this

I know I'm not

actually talking to someone

But I look pretty crazy and

I know it's super annoying for my son

who is thirteen (now fifteen) and easily embarrassed

to have a mom talking to herself

gesturing and making facial expressions

and a conversation which she's having with herself

when you're sitting right beside her

in the front seat of the car

Kind of weird. Yep. That's me. Bye.

Spoken 2013

Recorded this in 2013 when my son was thirteen. He's fifteen now. Yes, I was driving at the time, but had both hands on the wheel. No excuse, still distracting no doubt, not that I wouldn't be talking to myself aloud anyway, because I do. Just thought I may as well record myself. What the hell.

***

I Am Ashamed

I'm ashamed. Ashamed of the dust. Ashamed of the clutter. Ashamed that I do not, that somehow I cannot, bring myself to keep my house clean.

This afternoon, as I sat working at our dining room table, my husband just touched the dusty lamp above me, and I started coughing, choking, asthmatic that I am.

My son suffers with eczema, with asthma, as do I. Still, I leave the dust undisturbed, afraid of another asthma attack.

Too ashamed to ask for help. Too ashamed to hire help. Too ashamed to let anyone in. Too overwhelmed to attack the job myself.

Now my husband Nick chokes and coughs himself, as he cleans the lamp of its dust. Thank you, Nick, for all that you do.

***

Bipolar Disorder and Rewiring the Brain

My experience with psychotherapy supports the findings that we can "re-wire our brains." In cognitive therapy, I learned to stop negative thoughts and suicidal ideation, rewrite those thoughts and replace them with more accurate ones. In therapy, I've learned to reframe my life experiences as meaningful, as preparing me to be a better mother, wife, and daughter, and effective mental health advocate. Today I use the skills and insight I've gained in psychotherapy and medication to maintain my mental health.

***

Happy Anniversary

My husband and I have been married for nineteen years, together for twenty-two. Marriage is not always easy. We've weathered hard times. Well worth it. He has my back. Life is hard. Living with a mental illness makes it even more challenging. Helps to have someone there for emotional and physical support, someone to make sure we eat dinner, someone who can fix just about anything. He's an engineer. Quite handy around the house.

***

Distracted Driving

VIDEO TRANSCRIPT

My sister made me promise not to drive and videotape myself at the same time because that is driving while distracted. There's one problem with that, and that's that I'm more distracted when I don't articulate my thoughts. Because they race through my head, and I can only speak or write so quickly.

No matter how quickly I speak or how fast I type or write, it's not nearly as fast as my thoughts. And, it actually slows me down. So, I am less distracted. Hard to understand if you don't have thoughts that go really fast. Thoughts that are kind of a press of ideas. Too much. Too much. So anyway, that's it.

***

Mental Illness and Violent Acts

Some mass shootings are perpetrated by people with untreated mental illness. I've had to stop myself from doing violent things. I've had completely horrifying thoughts and impulses, which I've had to tell myself not to act on, had to harness all my self-control to not do. I have fought murderous (and postpartum incestuous and cannibalistic) thoughts and impulses. At the time, I was amazed that more murders and violent acts *don't* occur (and more infants not eaten).

***

I Got Out of the House This Week!

My major achievement this week was to get out of the house TWICE for ME, not just driving my son to and from school or caring for my parents.

MONDAY: OC WRITERS WRITE-IN

Monday, I attended an OC Writers write-in where I wrote 3282 words freely. The words need editing. They need shape. They possibly need to be fictionalized. Not sure.

WEDNESDAY: BRAIN DISEASE ADVOCACY

Yesterday I had a lovely lunch with Mary Palafox of FEDUP - Brain Disease Advocacy. FEDUP4Brain advocates uniting mental and physical health under ONE health care delivery system. Stop treating serious mental illnesses -- such as schizophrenia and bipolar disorder -- differently than other brain disorders.

***

Gaping Maw

I am a gaping maw. A wide-open gaping maw of unending unquenchable need. I feel that if I ever opened that maw, if I ever asked for help, if I ever showed my true self, my need, my pain, it is so great that I would scare off others, so great that no one could deal with it, so great that no one could love me.

If I let others, even my husband, see my true need, my true pain, my true self, they would run off in terror. So, I protect myself with a shield, a facade of strength. I don't let people close, not really. I just seem to. Actually, I hold everyone at arms-length. I let no one, not even myself, access to my true self, to my deepest pain, to my longing, to not feeling lovable, to not feeling truly able to love. I hold back always.

I may appear one way and feel quite another. I appear capable and loving, but feel like a failure, never quite measuring up, never earning something that always should have been offered unconditionally.

***

Arm's Length

My psychiatrist has asked me numerous times how my sister has handled my parents differently than I have. How has she protected herself? How has she kept herself from being so enmeshed in the family dynamic?

The answer is that my sister says no. She keeps my parents at arm's length. She didn't answer the phone whenever my mother called, letting it go to voicemail instead. She didn't let my mother pry and control her. And, she never identified with them.

I, on the other hand, was a member of the first-born club. My mother, father, and I were all first-born. I was repeatedly told that I was like them in that I, too, was first-born. I, like them, was a type-A personality, an over-achiever, a workaholic.

I shouldered higher expectations. I was to be a doctor or a lawyer. My goal was to be a neurosurgeon. In high school, I almost got straight A's, ranking third in a class of 450. I assumed that I would go to an Ivy League school and was devastated when I wasn't accepted.

My parents graduated at the top of their high school classes and were high achievers in college. My mother was captain of her college debate team. My father earned two bachelor's degrees in five years, one in chemical engineering and one in humanities. Years later, living off savings while supporting a wife and two daughters, he attended Harvard Business School.

I expected to out-achieve them. I didn't. I failed. I fell apart. I couldn't withstand the strain, the expectations, the speed of being a UCLA honors biochemistry major.

I wanted a well-rounded education and to have fun, so I dropped out of the second quarter of honors chemistry. Physics and biology, too, I only took one semester each. Honors calculus, though, I loved and took for the entire year. Math was always my favorite subject and I regret not continuing my math studies.

Bottom line: I must say NO. I must STOP identifying with my parents. I must learn to hold my parents at arm's length. I must learn to be a "good enough" daughter, and not try to live up to any real or perceived expectations.

***

Bipolar, Rage & Violence

Sure, having a mental illness does not mean that you will be violent. Still, some of us with mental illness, myself included, do have or have had violent thoughts and impulses. For the most part, I have not acted on mine, at least not the worst of them. I have raised my voice, flipped the dinner table, and thrown my iPad. Some people, like me, need treatment to control violent thoughts and impulses.

***

Folie à Deux

I AM MY MOTHER

Caveat: Please understand that delusional thought processes are SYMP-TOMS of mental illness. I feel compassion, even as I feel pain and anger, as someone negatively affected by parental delusional thoughts. I, too, have experienced delusional thoughts and bizarre impulses. I'm heir to familial mental illness. I get it.

With great trepidation I wrote the original version of this piece for publication with the *Feminine Collective* at *femininecollective.com/folie-a-deux*. Will I hurt those I love? Probably. Is it worth it to tell the truth, to let people know what it is like to live under the shadow of unacknowledged, untreated mental illness? I pray that the good outweighs the pain. I pray for understanding and compassion.

Mental illness, when untreated and unacknowledged, can cause great pain to extended family members. Out of respect for my relatives, this version has been changed. The actual content of my mother's bizarre delusions is masked to protect those she attacked.

***

This is my story, my perspective, my understanding.

Folie à Deux

Taboo content

Folly of two

Folly, delusion, shared by my parents

I've protected them

Partly out of respect

Partly out of fear of the repercussions

Partly, for my sister who is protective of their privacy

We grew up under the shadow of a bizarre distorted thought process

Symptomatic of mental illness

Originated by our mother

Backed up by our father

In front of us, since we were young

Our mother would attack our father

Making bizarre claims with no basis in reality

My sister and I would look across the table

For our reality check

No. Where did she get these bizarre ideas?

There was no evidence for them

They made absolutely no sense

Our mother was crazy

Yes, I am heir to her illness

After our mother would verbally abuse our father

In front of us, her daughters

With unfounded claims of bizarre content

Content from her mind, her thought process, with no basis in fact

She would storm off to her bedroom

Leaving our father with us

Then he, our father, made us apologize to our mother

We would ask why, for we hadn't done anything wrong

Mom had been abusive to HIM

We just witnessed our mother's attack

We did nothing wrong

He would respond that

She just didn't feel appreciated

She needed our attention

He would throw us under the bus

Use us as his buffer

Not only NOT protect us, but use us

My father would join my mother in her belief system

That thought process, that dynamic

Put a wedge between the outside world and us

Between our extended family and us

My sister and I didn't even go to our paternal grandparents' funerals

For fear of how our mother would react

She would have considered it a betrayal

I've had to tread carefully over the years

As I've befriended my paternal extended family over Facebook

I know my mother is sick and my father joined her

I once saw an old home movie of my mother

She danced in circles around the rest of her family

I saw myself in her

Twirling rapidly around others as they simply stood still

Sh t, I thought. I am my mother.

But with one major difference

I got help

Only later, through therapy, did I realize that our mother's attacks on our father was abusive to US--for we, as children, and later as teens, should never have been privy to bizarre delusions.

***

DEAR READER: Boundaries, Intimacy, and Trust

My post published today on *Organic Coffee, Haphazardly* at *haphazardcof-fee.com/2016/11/01/dear-reader-boundaries-intimacy-and-trust/*

Yes, I have boundary issues.

Email and direct messages, especially Facebook direct messages, intrude. I do not feel safe in the secretive world of chat. I need witnesses, others protecting my back. I prefer communication public, on my Facebook timeline or as comments to my blog posts.

People, you can comment on my timeline, which is public! Stop interrupting my solitude. Stop direct messaging me.

Similarly, I hate phone calls. I swear when the telephone rings. Not able to simply ignore it and let it go into voicemail. The ringing irritates me and provokes a response. I must pick it up. But, if it's a fax, a computer-generated call, market researcher, or telemarketer, I hang up on them. They are not welcome. Period.

My boundary issues date back to my relationship with my parents. You see, I grew up in an enmeshed alcoholic family. My sense of proper boundaries is off.

My way of coping is to flash my soul, then retreat. Never really letting anyone close. Always holding others at bay, at arm's length.

I either flee or swamp. Flee from advances, from intimacy. Swamp and overwhelm with my intensity, with my attention, as if I'm stalking, though that is not my intent.

I've been told I'm too intense. That behavior of mine can scare others. I've even been blocked due to my zeal in following and commenting.

Why bother to write this, to share this with you, my reader? Am I trying to find a better balance? Do I feel I must explain myself and my behavior to others? Do I feel guilty that I have hurt people with my sometimes cold, sometimes distant behavior? With my inconsistency? Do I consider myself a cold bitch?

Perhaps I'm working my issues out in a public forum, in front of an audience. Perhaps I am the narcissist my son recently claimed me to be.

Ultimately, though, I need to communicate, to share a message. I need to write and speak publicly for I am by nature a communicator, an orator, and a theatrical performance artist. At the same time, I must maintain some sense of privacy and solitude, a safe zone.

***

Fragile

feeling

fragile

as if

I will

break apart

into a

thousand

pieces

***

Yes, I'm a Math Geek

WARNING: HERE, I BOAST

In my youth, I was more a lover of math concepts than numbers. No longer do I get to use my beloved unit circle or calculus. My one regret is not continuing math past honors calculus, a class I loved. I love to boast (yes, I'm still proud of this achievement) that I, at eighteen, got 100 percent on the math placement exam at UCLA.

Today, at fifty-three, I'm far from that sharp-as-a-tack, hypomanic young woman. Wiser, perhaps, but time (and neglect) has taken a toll on my mind and my body.

Time to Care for Myself

Yesterday I saw my internist. In the last year and a half, I've gained twenty pounds and my triglycerides are high. Haven't been eating well, especially for my needs, as I have SIBO, small intestinal bacterial overgrowth. Trust me, you don't want the details. Many people with IBS (irritable bowel syndrome) have SIBO. To control my symptoms, I must keep to a restrictive low FODMAP diet (fermentable oligosaccharides, disaccharides, monosaccharides and polyols), which involves not eating many healthy foods, like onions, garlic, pit fruit (who doesn't love peaches?).

Time to get moving, too, for I haven't been exercising. Both exercise and diet are important for mental and physical health. My mother and my maternal grandmother both had strokes, which puts me at risk. Exhaustion keeps me from exercising, which reinforces the feeling of exhaustion.

My focus has been on caring for others: my parents and my son.

Time to care for myself.

***

Am I Still a Mental Health Blogger?

What defines being a blogger, specifically a mental health blogger? Must I write regularly or frequently? Must I always write about mental health? What if that is not my focus ALL the time? What if I'm so busy that living with bipolar disorder is not in the forefront of my mind? What if I'm overwhelmed by my life circumstances? What if I'm simply taking a break?

I'm not the most disciplined writer. Never been one for discipline; though, I do brush and floss my teeth every night. My house is a mess, dusty and cluttered. I bathe or shower (I prefer to bathe) at least once a week. (You are probably disgusted by this admission. I try not to move too much, so I don't sweat and get stinky. Yes, I know I should exercise daily. And, eat better. Just because I know better, doesn't mean I do better.)

Followers of my blog say they miss me when I write once a month, and not more often. Not sure if it's nice to be missed, or if it's stressful, if I have an obligation to write.

No, I have no obligation to write.

That's why I blog.

It's mine. All mine.

Yes, I interact with others here and enjoy doing so. I respond to those who comment.

Recently, though, I've been busy with life. My illness, bipolar disorder, hasn't been the focus of my blog. I'm fairly stable. My symptoms are more or less in remission. But, the concepts of remission and recovery can mislead. Serious mental illnesses, like bipolar disorder and schizophrenia, are chronic, lifelong brain disorders. You can live with them. Medications can help you treat the symptoms. But the brain disorder remains.

To stay stable, I must be careful. I must plan for how certain circumstances affect me.

Last month I presented, and next week I again will present, as an individual living with mental illness for NAMI Provider Education, at the hospital where more than a decade ago (12 years now) I was treated two weeks inpatient, and for a few months in their partial hospitalization program until I got bored.

I get overstimulated in social situations and must recover. I cannot sustain that level of social functioning without paying a high price: psychiatric instability, hypomania and subsequent depression, mood cycling. So, I must keep in mind that I will need downtime afterwards, time to recover.

So, I started writing this piece wondering about the effects of my recent lack of "mental health" blog posts. I've also slacked off reading and commenting on others' blogs. Sorry, folks.

I've been too busy doing taxes (scanning tons of receipts), driving my son to and from school and numerous doctors' appointments (unfortunately, he isn't motivated to get his driver's license anytime soon and knows we didn't get ours until we were eighteen and nineteen), and making sure my parents are happy.

When I haven't been busy, I've been exhausted, too exhausted to write, to read, to do anything verbal. Instead, I took up doing jigsaw puzzles on my iPad. I enjoy that they are visual, non-verbal, and engage my mind.

***

Spring Brings Hypomania

This year, as winter has ended, and spring has begun, I've taken it slowly and protected myself from overstimulation. You have not heard from me as much, as I've not been as active writing here or on social media.

You see, springtime triggers hypomania in me. Now I'm experiencing mild hypomania, irritability, and some mixed features. I feel myself internally crying, and on the verge of tears. I have good reason to cry, but my feeling of emotional vulnerability and instability goes beyond my current life circumstances. Perhaps, for I've never experienced losing my parents to dementia, while raising a chronically ill teenager, and living with bipolar disorder. Sounds pretty stressful.

My response is to cocoon, to reduce stimulation, to take sleep meds if I must, to reduce stress. When I haven't been busy caring for my son or visiting my parents, I've relaxed and let my husband spoil me.

Hopefully I'll feel much better once tax season is over. Exhausting and stressful.

***

Rejected

Just got rejected by an online psychotherapist. Ouch. Slap in face. No doubt because of my bipolar diagnosis. I understand that online therapy is not always appropriate. The therapist in question may not have had the proper background and training.

Still, it hurts, and I remain, I don't know, vulnerable? Feeling in need of support, specifically psychological support.

My psychiatrist, with whom my psychotherapist works, runs weekly group therapy, which I used to attend. But I don't do well in groups. My boundaries are poor. I take care of others and don't get enough support for myself. I'm selfish right now and know that I need the undivided attention of a psychotherapist. I need some healing. Badly.

Honestly, my fantasy is to go on a therapeutic retreat. Something like a spa weekend but including sessions with a licensed psychologist with expertise in bipolar disorder (which is a serious mental illness). Must maintain coping mechanisms. Cannot fall apart.

***

Thank You, Treatment Team

Assuming that my therapist was not available, I called my psychiatrist to see if he was available. He was! Yay!

My psychiatrist saw me, listened to me, and reassured me that it sounds like I'm exhausted, which is understandable considering all that I've done in the last year and a half.

My therapist happened to be there when I visited, and I learned that she had a cancellation next week. Double yay! Now I don't have to wait until the end of the month to see her.

My psychiatrist reminded me that group therapy was always available for me to rejoin.

Anyway, before I got through to my team, I decided to take a couple of days off. Not exactly on a nature retreat. Just staying in a local hotel overlooking our local toll road (which is LOUD). Not as nice as I had hoped.

Maybe I'll check out tomorrow and find somewhere quieter for my second night "away."

***

Silent Lately

I haven't written in a while, nor have I read or commented on others' posts. I used to write brief reviews after reading a book. Recently, I've simply left stars.

Why? Because I simply needed to recover. Recovering not from an episode of bipolar disorder (though I do live with that illness and must take care of myself), but from exhaustion, physical illness, and the demands of life.

Sometimes I need silence. Sometimes I must do less. I must NOT do.

Since my mother's stroke in November 2015, I've had added responsibilities overseeing my parents' finances and care. My sister helps me make decisions and offers emotional support, but she lives in another state and has her own life to live.

I parent a high-needs adolescent who gets sick A LOT and has struggled throughout his life with migraines, ADHD, depression, and anxiety.

My husband, son, and I have all been sick.

All this weighs on me.

So, I've pulled back.

I've been silent.

I've binge-watched TV.

I've done lots of jigsaw puzzles on my iPad.

Starting Monday, I'm hiring my neighbor, who has been a caregiver to seniors, to help me with my chaotic physical environment. Together, we will organize and clean my house. It's cluttered and dusty. The floors and refrigerator need cleaning. Hopefully, that will improve both our physical and emotional health.

***

Hypomania Raises Its Head (Again)

Last Tuesday in therapy, I said I no longer felt hypomanic. At the time, I seemed relaxed, at ease. By Wednesday my mind was racing. At night, when it was time to fall asleep, to slow down my mind, instead of thinking in my usual monologue, as an orator narrating my life, I heard a cacophony of voices.

I wondered if, when those voices crowded my mind, I should have written them down to see if I was thinking in dialogue. Were the voices characters wanting to be heard, auditory hallucinations, or thoughts racing so fast, I could not make heads or tails of them? Most likely speeding thoughts.

When I couldn't fall asleep, instead of writing, I medicated myself to sleep. I force sleep when it won't come on its own.

As I wrote last week during the day, while my son attended school, I could not hear the noise. Instead, I focused on my voice and that's what I thought. Writing disciplined my thoughts.

***

Sick of It

Tired of writing memoir. Not just sick of writing about my mental illness, sick of living the same struggles day after day. Do not want to end my life. Far from suicidal. Just want to end my symptoms. I'm WAY over it. Sick of being sick.

***

Walking the Line

Living with bipolar is like walking a tightrope, trying to maintain my balance, fearful of each step I take.

As a young adult, I didn't understand what triggered my highs and lows. I saw depression as a problem, but I didn't fully understand the role of workaholism, overachievement, and perfectionism, even as I crashed over and over.

After my training as a clinician, when I finally turned to medication for help, I understood and described myself as cyclothymic (experiencing less extreme highs and lows than bipolar) even as I was diagnosed and treated for dysthymia (persistent depression).

At almost 54, I'm still learning about myself. I used to consider myself extroverted. I threw parties, loved to be on stage and the center of attention. When I look back, though, I performed at parties. I did not really feel comfortable. I danced and laughed loudly, or I shrank back into a corner, wanting to leave.

Now social stimulation overwhelms me. Sounds bombard me.

This summer, first the long days challenged me with too much sunshine. My thoughts raced at bedtime. I found it hard to sleep, had to take benzodiazepine to turn off my thoughts and allow slumber. I started to ramp, to take on more and more tasks.

Recently, I signed a three-month private trainer contract at a Pilates studio. The training itself overstimulates me. Too much social interaction. The exercise has aggravated forgotten knee and hip injuries. I know that Pilates should help, but for now, I'm in pain.

Responding to the pain, I've scheduled appointments with an orthopedist and a physical therapist.

Escape is what I crave. I want so badly to be in a less stimulating place, quieter, slower, surrounded by trees on one side to shelter me, and an open vista on the other so I can look at the horizon and feel free. It's a place I've had in my imagination a long time. My husband and I have been talking, but it's not yet time to retire. Our life is here for now.

***

Bipolar & Dementia

I fear dementia. Both of my parents have dementia and live in a memory care community. They love one another and seem happy where they are now, but it took a while to make that happen. They wanted to maintain their independence. Understandable.

I fear dementia. Though I hope by avoiding alcohol and taking my bipolar medications, I can prevent it. (Alcohol is a neurotoxin, and I have a family history of alcoholism.)

Still, I fear a downward spiral. That fear I want to overcome. Face it. Stand up to bipolar disorder and dementia. Take care of my brain.

Even if my bipolar disorder progresses, even if I get dementia, I can still love and be loved, just as my parents still love and are loved.

***

Hypomania, Praise, and Self-Talk

The praise came. Kitt loved to please. The more praise she received, the better she felt. The more she achieved, the higher she soared, until she couldn't. Her body couldn't keep up. She broke down, couldn't get out of bec, and beat herself up for falling, for failing.

WRITE WITH PURPOSE

Back in September 2013, my father-in-law fell seriously ill. Not only did I worry that we might lose him, but I realized that my parents were approaching the end of their lives. My fears regarding my father-in-law's health, its effect on my husband, and my aging parents' health led to anxiety and hypomanic racing thoughts.

To cope with those fears and racing thoughts I started writing online. My blog was born. Putting my hypomanic and anxious thoughts out there, I found myself in a mutually supportive community of mental health advocates and fellow writers.

What started as self-care to cope with hypomania and anxiety, as something I *HAD* to do to clear my mind of racing thoughts, has become purposeful over the course of writing at kittomalley.com. Readers responded to my writing. My writing helped them. We helped each other in sharing our stories.

Expressive writing is an excellent coping skill. The research of social psychologist James W. Pennebaker, PhD, indicates that expressive writing heals. A pioneer in writing therapy, Pennebaker has written self-help workbooks such as *Writing to Heal: A Guided Journal for Recovering from Trauma and Emotional Upheaval*.

You need not buy a book or start an online blog to write to heal, though. Just write. If you live with a serious mental illness, like bipolar disorder, use your writing in conjunction with medication and therapy, to recover, to cope.

At first, I wrote to heal, without even knowing that I was doing so. As a therapist, I knew that writing and art were healing; for years ago I gave the troubled teens I counseled journals. Now I write to educate, inspire, commiserate, join and support others. My purpose has grown. Now my writing is a tool for advocacy.

***

Writing History Trashed

At one point in the past year, in an attempt to de-clutter a hopelessly cluttered house, I tossed all of my letters, journals, papers, and essays into the recycling bin. Later, I regretted it and went to retrieve them, but the papers had gotten wet and dirty, so I left them. Some of it was probably worth keeping.

I feel like I've left the best of my brain behind. Like I will never again be as sharp or as brilliant. I've grown accustomed to my brain on valproic acid. Sluggish, forgetting words. Maybe someday I'll revive it, and once again be creative and thoughtful. Or, not.

***

Inspiration

So now that I am no longer hypomanic, the big question is, will I continue to write? Where will I get my inspiration without the push of manic thoughts and my need for catharsis?

***

To Blog or Not to Blog

Last week, as I started interviewing for part-time positions, I considered taking down my blog, worried that I would be found out and that prospective employers would avoid hiring me, fearing the worse. We hear of nightmares on the news, of mentally ill who did not receive adequate treatment and did unthinkably violent things. My blog remains. I still am what a dear friend calls a "dancing, naked muse." Figuratively, of course.

I believe that I have a calling to inform, to write, and to speak (when and how I speak, I do not know) about what it is like to be mentally ill, what it is like to be very bright and seemingly capable, but struggling to cope. I see myself speaking publicly, but do not know how to do so, how to find my audience, my stage, my dais.

For now, the most important role I serve is as mother to my thirteen-year-old son, who wants me at home afternoons, evenings, and during the summer.

***

Fill the Space with Words

The name of the writer's workshop that I plan to attend is "Sit Down, Shut Up, and Write." Can I do so? When overstimulated by social contact, I tend to talk, to take over. Can I channel that into writing? Will I push people away with arrogance? Will I charm them? Can I just sit down, shut up, and write?

Here is what I fear I may do or look like: over-intellectual prig, snob, condescending bitch, insecure, scared, incompetent do-nothing, leech, poor mother, poor wife. Okay, now the tables have rapidly changed. Went from high to low. Mixed episode. Scared, insecure girl behind smarty-pants façade?

***

Do I Need an Editor?

Do I need an editor? Do I need to organize my writing into a more cohesive whole? Or, does this format fit what I am trying to accomplish? What is it I am trying to accomplish? I believe that I have a ministry to educate others on mental illness, specifically bipolar disorder.

I see myself writing and speaking. Not just to other writers, or to others struggling with mental illness, but to the world at large. Perhaps, in part, for narcissistic reasons. I am, and have always been, a drama queen. I love an audience. I need fawning fans. Still, I see the need for more education about mental illness. We do not all go about on violent rampages. We may think horrible thoughts, yet not act on them.

***

No More Grad School for Now

Okay, so the other night -- or maybe it was in the morning, I'm not sure -- through LinkedIn I checked out Fuller Theological Seminary's School of Psychology and their PhD program in psychology. Got to thinking, do I want to pursue a PhD integrating theology and psychology? What they are doing is what interests me, yet I do not want to be going to graduate school and paying tuition now when we are preparing for my son to go to

142

college in four years. Furthermore, I don't see myself studying. I see myself speaking and writing, which I can do now, using this format, other social media, and YouTube. Who knows what the future has in store.

***

Stepping Out and Meeting Up

Started going to group therapy and two writers' groups the last three weeks. Not sure how much "work" I can take on right now. Attending group therapy and the writers' groups is a big step towards leaving the isolation of my home, where I care for my son and husband, and going out into the adult world to socialize and engage in intellectual and creative pursuits. My goal first was to explore what happens to me amid social stimulation. As mentioned in my "Titrating Stimulation" post, social stimulation and social demands can trigger hypomania in me, so I must maintain healthy boundaries. Still, my goal has broadened. Now I see myself as a writer and an aspiring public speaker.

***

Prose Poems

In a way, I write prose poems. Short jabs of non-fiction. A few words indicating where my thoughts are, where they may take me. Do I communicate adequately in my terse interjections? Need I go into more detail? Can I? Does it suit me? Does it even matter? For now, I do not know. I just write these short posts and hope for the best, assuming they will lead me somewhere, that they will take on some life of their own, that someday, somehow, I may weave them into a greater whole. Perhaps, and then, perhaps not. Perhaps this blog is simply what it is and nothing more. These posts, these few words written here and there, communicate my thoughts as I have them, as I pull them out of my head and onto the page.

***

Advocate or Narcissist

Thursday, a new member of OC Writers, a writing group I attend, referred to my work as "changing the world." Of course, he hadn't yet read my blog. As a Christian author, he assumed my writing was altruistic, since described it as a mental health blog where I have also posted some seminary papers. The question on my mind is whether I truly help others in writing autobiographical posts, or rather whether I indulge in unfettered narcissism? Perhaps, only time will tell, if I can reach out and help others. This site serves both purposes. In writing I heal myself, overcome my isolation and challenge my intellect, as well as engage others, who, like me, struggle with mental illness, or seek an understanding of what it is like to live with mental illness. I'm not sure how well my theological writing meshes with those purposes. But I do know that I believe increasingly, more and more each passing day, that God has called me to perform a mental health ministry, and that in striking me down with bipolar disorder, and a stint in a psychiatric hospital, God forced me to quit working in the commercial real estate sector to take better care of myself, my sensitive son, and my husband.

***

144

Blustery Day

When driving my son to school, I commented that it was a blustery day. He responded, "No, it's the Apocalypse." With the temperatures approaching 100°F and the Santa Ana winds whipping through dry brush and parched trees, he may be closer to the truth. Southern California is on fire. This time in May. Way too early for wildfire season to begin. Wildfires rage in Carlsbad, Camp Pendleton, Long Beach, Anaheim, Santa Paula, Rancho Bernardo and Lompoc. Today, we live in a fiery oven.

***

Thanks on Father's Day

Tonight, as I sit beside my husband, watching videos of our son downhill mountain biking earlier today, I decided to express my gratitude in celebration of Father's Day. My husband is a private man, and on more than one occasion he has warned me not to boast. So, to keep my boasting to a minimum, and to maintain a modicum of privacy, I will keep my gratitude brief. My middle-aged husband is so dedicated and loving a father that he tries to keep up with our daredevil, just-shy-of-fourteen-year-old son, as they bicycle insanely steep expert-level mountain trails. Best of all, I love my husband, and he loves (dare I say, adores) me. Parenting is tough. Parenting while living with a mental illness, even harder. Parenting with a supportive, understanding spouse, the best thing ever. Thank you to the best father in the world (in my not so humble and very much boastful opinion).

***

Third Person

Once, a lifetime ago, when I was only twenty-eight, a rather gifted poet friend of mine, upon reading the first-person narrative of my journal, suggested that I try writing in third person. I gave it a try and in so doing turned my rather self-absorbed, navel-gazing journal writing into fiction. Someday, some year, I may do it again. I may write fiction, or at least a highly fictionalized version of my life. Who knows?

Like how I envision myself someday an orator, I see before me possibilities. Possibilities in the not-too-distant future. I have certain gifts, such as public speaking (preaching, actually), writing, and perhaps once again helping, and healing others as a psychotherapist. I must cultivate these gifts and at some future date use them. In the meantime, I wait patiently, carefully taking life as it comes, one step at a time, one day at a time. For now, I still very much need my time and energy devoted to caring for myself, my son, and my husband. Everything else can wait.

***

As a Child

As a child I wanted to be a doctor

To cure people of disease

As a teen I wanted to be a neurosurgeon

To fix brains with a scalpel

As a young woman

I became a psychotherapist

To fix troubled youth with broken lives

With the exchange of spoken words

I kept falling apart

My brain was broken

My thoughts self-loathing or racing

My emotions unbearably intense

Over and over

I sought and received help

First with psychotherapy

Later with medicine

Today I remain a broken woman

Still healing, still learning

Today I use words, written words, spoken words

To touch, heal, and teach others

Or so I hope

***

Why Do I Write?

I write, for I am more than a mother and a wife. I am a writer. I write, for I must. I write to keep my brain from atrophying. I write to capture those speeding thoughts. I write to pull myself out of soul-sucking lethargy. I write to give voice to my experience. I write to fight stigma against those who live with mental illness. I write to acknowledge that my life has meaning. I write, for it is a calling, for I have a purpose, a cause, a message to share. I write for validation of my message, that it has been received, that it has made a positive difference in someone's life. I write because I can.

***

Happy Anniversary!

Today is my one-year anniversary blogging. Hurray! The process of blogging, of writing, of networking with other writers both in "real life" and onl ne has shaped me over this past year. I now feel intellectually engaged, emotionally supported, purposeful and hopeful. Yes, hopeful. That is HUGE. I now have goals for the future that have grown out of my experience blogging as a mental health advocate. I can see those dreams coming to fruition. Pretty awesome, actually.

***

Time to Build a Book?

Yesterday I started to copy my blog content into Scrivener, "a powerful content-generation tool for writers that allows you to concentrate on composing and structuring long and difficult documents" (LiteratureandLatte. com). I had hoped I could simply export my WordPress blog into an xml document and then import it into Scrivener. Unfortunately, since I use Windows rather than the Mac OS, the best work-around I could find involved more advanced coding skills than I care to learn right now. Besides, perhaps the process of copying and pasting my posts and pages, including those never published, might inspire me, or at least jog my memory.

***

What Purpose Guides Me?

As I ask myself what purpose guides me as I pull content from my blog into Scrivener, I'm not so sure that I want to take on writing a book. Perhaps it is to create something else, not a memoir or rehashed blog, but an organized and cohesive call to action for mental health. This call to action need not be a book, perhaps blogging better suits me. Scrivener enables me to quickly and easily organize my blog writing, and possibly rewrite and repurpose old posts that still have merit.

149

***

Language Frustrates Me

For Throwback Thursday, I am posting something I wrote about thirty years ago when I was as an undergraduate. I would submit it as a writing sample when I applied for jobs.

Language frustrates me. Because of it, I think in distinctions; I draw lines where they do not in fact exist; I categorize and differentiate. All this I do to simplify, to impose order. All this so that I need not think or feel or know too much. All this so that I may function in a complex world. Otherwise, I would be overwhelmed. Or so I believe. But, in actuality, my attempts to simplify, to order the world around me, make my world more complex. More complex because I distort. More complex, for language is inherently imprecise. And, I get caught in my errors, in my ignorance and in my arrogance. I err when I oversimplify. I close my eyes to what is really going on when I ignore subtleties that elude definition. And, I arrogantly play God when I try to control my environment, imposing on it an order that is not necessarily there. Still, I convince myself that making these distinctions somehow empowers me. But the definitions, the distinctions, the categorizations I make become cages, and I find myself, not the objects I define, behind the bars. For in limiting what is limitless, in trying to contain what will not fit into any box or cage, I limit and imprison myself.

This piece of prose poetry means a great deal to me. It still resonates. Retyping it now makes me question why I would submit it as a writing sample for legal assistant, counseling, and business positions. The piece is perhaps a bit too telling. Guess I've always been an open book. My questioning and open nature, my love for ideas, my ambivalence for language, my theological bent, are part and parcel of who I am. Have been and still are.

Too bad I didn't save more of my writing, that I pitched it all to clean house. This piece, though, I kept in my résumé file.

Christmas Day

So here I am on Christmas Day, at a loss for words. Somewhat over-whelmed and physically exhausted. We've fought a stomach bug for far too long. Just as you think you are better, it comes back and slaps you down. In any case, Santa stuffed the adults' stockings with some yummy gourmet goodies. I've already eaten my chocolate bar from the stocking. Doesn't matter how sick I feel, I'll inhale chocolate, even as I grow sicker and sicker as I consume it. Yes, I'm a chocoholic.

****

Journaling and Saying No

New Year's Eve. Been awhile since I've journaled hard copy with pen in hand. Not sure how long this will last. So, what is it that I need to write down here? I have no idea. I have no idea what brings me here – pen to paper. I write in the dark with my husband beside me asleep and my son down the hall. I use a small hand-held reading light.

Not sure if I am doing anything of value now. But at least these are MY words. I am not simply sharing someone else's words, someone else's message. Perhaps that is something that I must do, for sometimes when I read someone else's writing, I'm struck by how amateurishly it was writ-ten. I know that I can write better. [Forgive me for my arrogance, but I was

151

journaling, after all.]

I like my writing voice, when I unleash it. So, that I must. My voice is not corporate, though the materials I quote are. So, I feel this push to share to comment, to inform. It takes up all my time.

I'm doing it again: work. And what do I when I work? I subsume my own needs, quiet my own voice, ignore my own needs, for the needs of the whole. Wouldn't it be wonderful if I could instead develop MY voice? Focus on my writing? Perhaps it is time to   read, follow and comment less. Perhaps it is time to blog more. To speak. To write. To focus.

***

Taking the 101

Now, after having blogged for about one year and four months, I'm finally taking the `WordPress Blogging University` course, *Blogging 101: Zero to Hero*. Today's assignment is to write and publish a post about who I am and why I'm here. Here goes. Obviously, my name is Kitt O'Malley. I mean, my name is at the top of the page, in the URL, tied to a bazillion or so social media presences, so that is who I am. As my tag line implies, I live with a diagnosis of bipolar disorder. To find out more about who I am, you can read About Kitt, My Story, or read about my "mystic" psychotic break.

The prompts for today's post are:

Why are you blogging publicly, rather than keeping a personal journal?

I blog publicly (but I've also started to journal again) because I have a message to share. Blogging can be a powerful way to affect change – both positive social change and personal change. I started my blog because of a trigger to mood cycling. I found myself blogging for I felt a pressure to write, to get thoughts and words out of my mind. Why share them publicly? Well, I suppose I need support, I need an outlet, I need an audience. I greatly enjoy the company and mutual support in the blogosphere, especially in the mental health blogging community.

There is a strong community of mental health bloggers who offer each other positive support. My focus has become clearer as I have written, and as I have engaged with other bloggers. I am a mental health advocate. I am a member of a community of mental health advocates. We not only offer each other support, but we educate each other and the public about mental health issues, and work to overcome social stigma attached to mental illness.

What topics do you think you'll write about?

From my answer above, you can pretty much deduce that I write about mental health, specifically about living with bipolar disorder, but I do not limit myself to that subject. I have written about other subjects, and I sometimes I take photographs, mostly of flowers, which I occasionally post.

Who would you love to connect with via your blog?

I would love to connect with anyone seeking a better understanding about bipolar disorder, those living with bipolar disorder, and those who love someone with bipolar disorder. In writing and rewriting the previous sentence, I realized that my primary focus is bipolar disorder more than other mental illnesses; though, I do disseminate information about mental illness in general, especially when sharing information from the National Alliance on Mental Illness (NAMI) or the National Institute of Mental Health (NIMH).

If you blog successfully throughout the next year, what would you hope to have accomplished?

Write to advocate, educate, destigmatize, and support about mental health issues. Hone my writing voice. Write more often and more prolifically. Maybe start weaving together what original content I have written into a book. Who knows?

***

I do not whisper. I ROAR.

Motherhood transformed me. My identity changed. Now it changes again. I have constantly reinvented myself.

As a pre-med biochemistry major at UCLA, I was miserable and suicidal. Then I studied part-time at a community college, biding time to find my direction. Finding a niche as a legal studies major at UC Berkeley, I tried to reconcile my inner turmoil with very high professional aspirations.

First, I worked as a legal assistant, then went to graduate school, earned a master's in psychology and became a psychotherapist, only to crash and burn. Recovering from that breakdown, I re-entered the workforce as a temporary file clerk in the commercial real estate industry, where I had ten years of success.

Trying to balance work with motherhood, I failed miserably, and ended up hospitalized in a psychiatric unit with rapid cycling and mixed symptoms of bipolar disorder. After months of partial hospitalization, I became a reluctant stay-at-home mother on disability.

What does an overeducated and reluctant stay-at-home mother with a recurring sense of calling (or a manic and delusional symptom of bipolar disorder, depending on one's perspective) do with her mind? Why, attend seminary, of course, which I did on two separate occasions, and on two separate occasions had to quit, due to symptoms.

Here I am writing my story again. To what end? To reinvent myself once again, not as someone who is ill, but as someone who fights, and loves, and writes, and has hope that new chapters of her life lie ahead.

I have a voice that must be heard. I have a message to share, and share it I do. I am not just my son's mother. I am not my diagnosis. I am able. I am able to affect change. I wield power. I am a mover and a shaker. I do not whisper. I ROAR.

***

Meaning of Life

I really have no idea if divinity truly exists. I do know that it is very human to look for and attribute meaning. Meaning is what I seek. Meaning is what I find. Whether or not that meaning really exists? I do not know. I question. I seek.

***

So Easily Broken

All around her books, binders, and training manuals piled. She had an article to finish and submit, blog posts to write, book reviews to complete, once she finished reading the books, and multiple social media presences to maintain. "Shit," she thought, "how the hell am I going to get out from under all this?" Why, oh, why had she made so many friends who wrote books and blogs she now felt obligated to read? Actually, she really wanted to read those books and blog posts. Really, she did. But there were only so many hours in the day, so many days in the week, so many weeks in the month, and she could not procrastinate indefinitely – actually, she could, and she did.

Why now had she decided to volunteer in her community? Volunteer work that required her to study densely written manuals before her actual training even began. Volunteer work in which she would bare her soul, expose her vulnerabilities – her struggles living with mental illness, with bipolar disorder – in public, in person, in front of classrooms of high school students, in front of mental health professionals. Yes, she would share her triumphs, too, but she didn't feel particularly triumphant amid the chaos that surrounded her. Her anxiety grew. She neglected herself, her family, her dogs, her home, even her roses.

Like she didn't have enough to do already. Everywhere she looked, on every horizontal surface, every counter, table, desk, chest of drawers, she saw clutter. In the corners of the master bedroom, under the stairs, on the living room and dining room floors, clutter. Stuff, and more stuff. The clutter needed sorting, needed decisions made. Keep or toss? Where would she put it, anyway? The clutter overwhelmed her – buried her.

Then there were those unfinished walls, patchworks of dreary earth tones the previous owner preferred, fresh new paint, and raw drywall texture covering up wounds from temper tantrums thrown. Turns out, not only toddlers throw temper tantrums. Her child had no way of knowing that if he kicked the wall it would break. Lesson learned. Walls are only sheetrock, son. They are not strong. They are not invincible. They are not all that solid. She felt just as fragile. Maybe she looked rock solid, but she was so easily broken.

***

I'm No April Fool

This admittedly amateurish attempt at April Fool's Day poetry (yes, that's rather heavy-handed alliteration; accept it, I like it, I'm on "A" roll) I originally wrote for *STIGMAMA.com*. I may not be a polished or proficient poet, but perhaps I am indeed a fool, perhaps, just perhaps, NOW THERE ARE TWO OF US. Even more likely, now there are far more than just the two of us fools. None of us is alone in our foolishness.

I'm No April Fool

Right now I'm half brain-dead

But I'm no April fool

Didn't always know this mind-fog

Still I'm no April fool

As I age my mind's not quite right

Am I now an April fool?

Wait and wonder when wisdom comes

Never comes, but memories fade

I'm no April fool

Or, am I?

***

Unlocking the Mind

How to get at the good stuff? Cannot even think of a better word for stuff!
Yes, I can look for a word using a thesaurus, which I probably will end up

do ng. But, for now, I'm very simply frustrated, for my mind has either been erased or is under lock and key. I'm reminded of what happens when I cannot recall a password and try time and time again to log on. After multip e tries, I'm locked out. No longer can I access a wealth of information at my fingertips. Locked out.

WRITING FIRST ASSIGNMENT

Twenty minutes to free write. Don't think about what you'll write. Just write.

Caveat: I must admit I edited what I wrote in the twenty minutes. Just cannot keep myself from rewriting...

Sir ce I already started writing and making an image for this assignment before I had even started the ass gnment, I guess I cheated. I also thought about what I was going to write and how I was going to go about it. Once again, not the assignment. Basically, I saw myself writing with interruptions. Interruptions because the dogs miss me, though they are sleeping on the floor right now. Interrupted expecting my son to ask for something, yet he remains ensconced in the guest room playing Xbox. He asked both last night and this morning whether and when I'd move the TV into his room because my sister and her family are visiting us tonight and tomorrow. But they won't be here until well after dinner, so we have plenty of time.

I imagined that my writing would somehow reflect my hypomanic mind. My mind is racing, but my writing tends (for the most part) to be organized. One reason is that I rewrite and rewrite and rewrite. Not for this project. This is stream of consciousness writing (I guess). Actually, I do not recall the exact meaning of stream of consciousness writing. Sounds rather ho-ity-toity and intellectual. This exercise and fingers flying, discussing the mundane, feels more like what the assignment calls free writing.

Okay, first interruption, quickly ignored. Poodle Coco nudged my left arm with his nose. He wanted to be petted. No pets right now. I'm FREE WRIT-ING. I'm being quite writerly. He circles me like a great white shark circling its prey, and then settles for kibble.

This morning I took a break - an interruption after my initial writing and before I copied and pasted the actual writing assignment up above. During that break I went to my local Starbucks to meet up with a fellow NAMI volunteer, mental health advocate, and mental health provider. Starbucks was crowded and loud, so I invited her over to my house. As it's messy and filthy, I'm proud of myself. Usually I'm too ashamed to have company over.

My timer just went off. Twenty minutes are up.

***

Two, No Three, Songs

Today's writing prompt was to think of three songs then free write about them. I came up with two. Two perfect songs. Both beautiful. Both worthy of life. Both true. Duke Ellington, I love. I've been a fan of his for decades. Perhaps since I was a young girl, as my father loved straight-ahead jazz and I inherited his passion for American Jazz. When I took private singing lessons, I studied the Ellington songbook. My fantasy was to be singing jazz standards in a slinky dress while on top of a grand piano. Rosemary Clooney's sexy voice and Ellington's band is perfect.

What better flip side to "Mood Indigo" than Pharrell's "Happy"? I feel both. I embrace both. I am a passionate woman. Not sure whether I will share this. Most likely I will. I tend to rewrite, to edit. Wonder if I will, or if I will simply let this go off into cyberspace.

Matters not to me, quite honestly. What does matter is that I explain, that I embrace the sad as well as the happy. I must take care of myself... blah, blah, blah... That's for my readers. Not for this exercise.

This exercise is about free writing. About unedited, uncensored writing. Oh, that's right. Just recalled there is a third song, "The Wall" by Pink Floyd. Yes, I was always a total geek and loved school, yet maintained what I consider to be intellectual defiance, or at least the ability to question authority while still following the law, the rules. My mind, I believe at least, is free. Yes, I've been traditionally educated in public schools. I'm thankful for my education. But, I remain in a way (perhaps), an iconoclast. I revel in my difference.

Give me a stage and I perform. I love it. I will speak up when no one else will. I do not fear consequences, for I believe that living by taking risks is more rewarding than living in fear without taking risks. So, yes, I disclose things that may expose me to... Cannot even think of the word. Let's just say to negative consequences.

The instance that I am thinking about right now involves me telling my son's guidance counselor and English teacher that I have bipolar disorder and have slapped my son, and that his assignment to speak in front of his class about a vignette from *The House on Mango Street* about child abuse with the requirement to connect the assignment to something in his life might hit too close to home.

I don't fear Children's Protective Services. I'm a very involved and motivated mother. I'm honest and open. I don't hide my errors. I don't lie. I work hard to be the best mother I can be. I have lots of documentation backing me up. I've been in therapy. My son has received help. We've gotten help as a family. I have professionals who have worked with us for more than a decade (not the same professionals, we have and do move, but we are back where we started, so the first professionals we saw as a family are still nearby). Anyway, those mental health professionals would no doubt vouch for our parenting, for my parenting.

So, I fear not.

Back to the songs... "Mood Indigo," "Happy," "The Wall."

I fear not sadness nor happiness. I feel both intensely. I need not conform. I need no thought control.

***

Gardening

Lightly pruned our fig tree this morning, evening out its limbs. May not have been the best time of year to prune it, but some branches grew out of control, reaching into the neighbor's yard and into the homeowners' association's hillside. Like me, the fig tree is productive, fecund, stretching itself outside the bounds of a narrowly defined suburban tract house's yard. Now it's basically a lollipop tree. Maybe it was better a bit unfettered.

The bougainvillea without doubt needs help, perhaps some light pruning. Not treating her correctly. I want a more robust plant, with colorful dense growth and less leggy limbs. Perhaps it gets too much water, its roots water-logged as they grow in clay and receive runoff from irrigated homeowners' association landscaping. The bougainvillea's not happy. She's drowning, as I sometimes feel I am underwater, overwhelmed with others' needs.

***

My Response to Laura A. Lord's "Of Roots and Wreckage"

Answering the call of Laura Lord's poetry

I write not as a poet

For I have not Lord's skill nor gift

But in response to her words moving mine

That, in itself, is testimony to how her words transport me

Her words take me to places I've never been

To experiences I've never had

But most of all

Her words move me to write in verse

Rather than in sentences and paragraphs

Perhaps there is no greater compliment

Than to say she inspires me

With her use of language

To hone my own

How

If only I could tell a story

As well as she does

Oh, well

By the way

I'm absolutely *thrilled* that she quoted me on her cover

I've read *ALL* of her books

***

Words Do Not Flow

Words do not flow.

I do not make the time to write, to free write.

I let myself atrophy, my brain numb.

What now? What do I have to say? To write?

Anything at all?

Or am I empty?

***

Still Insecure

I am not without self-doubt or self-loathing. I am both confident and inse-cure.

What do you think most people think about me? Middle-aged, fat, plain, sex-less. White privileged bitch.

Sometimes I feel good about myself, other times I do not. I am not as sexy as I once was.

I do not present myself as sexy, for that would be inappropriate. My son would die of embarrassment, and my husband prefers that I present that side of myself in private only to him.

I am aware that I am privileged. I know that. I look like the educated, upper middle-class suburban mother that I am. When I speak, I often use big words, which can be off-putting. Not everyone likes me. So be it.

***

Dissociation, Daydreaming, and Mind Dump

Already I've lost my place and forgotten what I was going to write. As I went to save this as a Word document to my hard drive, I saw some organizing I had to do, files in the wrong folder. Got to keep my data organized if not my home or my mind. At least this is something I can control or that I want to exert some control over.

So, what I was thinking and decided to get down on paper is how I enjoy daydreaming. I used to daydream or dissociate for hours a day while picking my skin, resulting in horrible sores on my face, chest, and arms. I enjoyed it. I enjoyed the picking and I enjoyed where my mind went. I did not enjoy the damage to my skin. That I was ashamed of. I would try to undo the damage with OTC treatments, with antibiotics, and cover it up with makeup. But the damage was done, and I have scars to show for it. Luckily my pock marks are relatively mild. My skin fair, so it does not scar as badly as skin with more melanin.

Why did I enjoy the daydreaming so? Because, quite simply, I love living in my head, in the world of ideas. I love imagining myself speaking to others. My thoughts often in the form of speeches or interviews. I am the one speaking or the one being interviewed. Suppose these imaginings are somewhat grandiose. Though, I believe that someday I will be doing some public speaking. Someday I will be the subject of interviews. Perhaps. Perhaps not.

One problem I have had, though, is that I'm often not sure if, in looking back, I simply thought something or if I told someone else that thought. That is, in the moment, I know that the conversation is simply in my mind. I'm under no delusion that it is taking place anywhere else at the time that I'm thinking it. But in retrospect, my memory is fuzzy, and I'm not sure whether I shared those thoughts with my husband or with someone else. Did I just think it? Or did I say it? If I did say it, to whom? I have no idea. Most of my ideas I keep in my head.

Though right now I'm writing them down. That I should do more of. Simply writing. Perhaps less reading of blogs and articles online and more writing of my thoughts as I think them.

I simply can't write what others want me to write. My blog, KittOMalley. com, is mine. My thoughts, my mind, my time, my blog, my social media activity.

If I'm to venture out of my house, off my couch, and work in the real world, I will not have the time to spend up to fourteen hours a day on social media. Perhaps some days up to sixteen hours. I know I spend an excessive amount of time and that it is not healthy. It is excessive. It is triggering of hypomania when I overdo it.

So, since I volunteered last week at NAMI Orange County and learned that someone recently resigned, my mind wrestles with the problem of data management for the position, and for the woman I volunteered for last week and will again tomorrow.

I love database design and find relational databases far better tools for managing data than spreadsheets. Spreadsheets are simply easier to use. Spreadsheets are the best tool for calculations. Numerical data. Relational databases are better for data for which there are complex relationships, one-to-many relationships, multiple relationships.

So, I may just publish this stream of writing, writing I did to empty my mind onto a page, into a Word document, as a blog post, and later take another look at designing a database, which users could access via a web browser and online login for NAMI Orange County's consideration.

***

Have I Fucked Up?

Okay, so now I'm wondering, have I fucked up? Am I not writing enough? Am I not engaging with my readers? How the fuck am I ever going to get anything done? It seems like I spend all my waking hours on the computer. Well, I actually DO spend virtually all my waking hours on my laptop, iPhone, or iPad. Still, I don't feel like I'm accomplishing what I want. I'm not writing enough. I feel like a hamster on a wheel. At what point do I simply cut back? What do I cut back? What do I continue to do? Help!

***

Have I Lost My Blogging Friends?

So, I've been busy, much busier than usual, in my real life, interacting with people in the flesh, which overstimulates me, so I haven't been reading and commenting on other blog posts like I usually do, like I used to do.

The posts I published Wednesday received few comments. I wonder, is it because I have let down my online community of mutually supportive readers by not reading and commenting on their posts? Or, is it because my posts were not personal or particularly original in nature, just a rehash of a conference I attended Friday and Saturday, and a repost of a TIME, Inc. infographic about why we still need Women's Equality Day? Perhaps my last post was simply too long (and boring, I now realize in going back and reading it).

I've been feeling guilty for not reading and commenting as much on other blogs, but I can only do so much, and taking care of myself comes first. I respond to comments on my blog. But, there are simply too many other blogs to read them all. I'm not even reading those with whom I've developed close online friendships.

Writing helps me. Consuming seemingly endless numbers of mental health posts, commenting on them and sharing them, unfortunately, does not. Perhaps doing so helps others, just not me. Not when I'm too overwhelmed. Not when I'm doing my best to slow down.

By the way, did some more in-person volunteering. Once again trying to figure this one out. How much in-person social interaction and volunteering I can take on without spinning like a hypomanic top?

Even an Electron has Purpose

She closed her eyes. She paused. She took a deep breath, meditated, waited to see where it would take her, where she would go, what she would feel.

She felt a great deep pain, a yearning, a desperate yearning, a deep, desperate yearning. Just that afternoon she was thinking, daydreaming, imagining herself pontificating, preaching, orating, explaining that she knew, that she could feel that we are all connected and all a part of something bigger, something so huge, yet so small, that even an electron had purpose.

Now how had she gotten there? She spoke of purpose. Of how each of us, no matter how small, even a single electron, has purpose, for it is part of the greater whole.

And now she, a part, a supposed part, a supposedly purposeful part of this greater whole, she yearned communion with this other. She felt apart from it. She yearned for it.

***

Thousands of Needles

She was a young girl

Living in a company compound

The only barrier between her

And the vast Arabian desert

A chain link fence

One day after school

A haboob, a desert sandstorm

Swept in through that flimsy fence

Thousands of needles

Drove into the thin skin

Of her face, arms and legs

She was not dressed

For the desert

She was dressed

As an American girl

Of the 1960s

In a sleeveless mini dress

She was blinded by the storm

By the flying needles of sand

When she opened her eyes

They stabbed her

When she shut her eyes

The grit remained

She could not see

She was lost in the storm

She had no idea where to go

What to do

Aside from wait

Even as an adult

Her memory is of

Thousands of needles

Stabbing her

Blinding her

Leaving her lost

Not of how it ended

Not of how or when the storm ended

Not of how or when she got out of the storm

***

A Room of My Own

Is it stigma to not mention that Virginia Woolf had mental illness (or had been sexually abused, for that matter)? Is that Woolf's legacy? Was she not far more than her illness, as are we?

Here's what I've been debating: removing my tagline, keeping references to bipolar in my bio and in my story, but not "limiting" my identity to someone living with bipolar or to be a mental health advocate.

I want to just write, to create art, to have that room of my own. Perhaps we need that locked door. Perhaps that metaphor can include, for some, privacy. Perhaps our illness does not limit us creatively, even as we struggle at times. Perhaps privacy is not stigma. Perhaps, for some, it is respect, it is a lock on a door which only the author, the artist, can open.

***

Where Am I Going Now?

Wife

Mother

Writer

Artist

Advocate

Activist

Speaker

Performer

Passionate

Empath

How do I describe myself? How do I best describe my blog? What has my blog become? What direction do I want to take it?

What direction is my life taking? Is my writing taking? Is my (dare-say) art or photography taking?

Back in the '90s, when I registered my first corporate URL, I knew that someday, some year, some decade, I would register the URL KittOMalley.com. I knew that I wanted to post my writing online.

I never envisioned KittOMalley.com as a community. Didn't realize that I'd be conversing with others. Never imagined what it has become.

***

Journal Writing

Here I write, not necessarily for my blog. No, I'm free writing for myself. Journaling. In the traditional sense. To ease my anxiety. To use some of the energy that my cup of coffee has juiced me with. I care not how I write. I try not to edit as I write. Instead, I write to let the tension flow out of my body, through my fingers and onto the page.

Somewhere in the back of my mind, I still write for an audience, not just for myself. Then again, I even daydream for an audience, as if I am performing, public speaking, addressing someone else. That's how I think. I am a performer at heart, ready to please, though I often do not – no, not often, sometimes. I sometimes do not please, even when I try, for I have little in the way of filter. The words come tumbling out, and sometimes I walk on toes, not meaning to.

Anyway, back to myself. Or perhaps not back to myself. What sort of writing would best help me now? A friend of mine, a former boyfriend, a poet, once suggested that instead of doing so much journaling in first person (which, yes, I've done over the decades intermittently), that I write in third person. Write as if I'm writing about a character. Distance myself from the content. Make it into a story.

Interesting idea. Not sure if I will do so now. But perhaps I will in the future.

***

Kitt's Invented Platitudes

I think it is human nature to ascribe or find meaning to events in our lives. Sometimes platitudes make us feel better. Sometimes worse.

My invented platitude: Nothing is always true, except when it is.

The platitudes I use regularly: You are loved. You are worthy of love. You are not alone.

Yet, at the same time, I can feel both so very alone and so very much a part of everything. Which leads me to another invented platitude: We are both alone and connected.

Even as I share my thoughts and feelings through words, I protect a part of myself, and do not let anyone completely in. No one really knows what it feels like to be me, but when I find others who seem to understand, something magic happens. I feel loved, supported, accepted. That feels good. That is what we do, what we can do, what we should do, for one another.

***

Travel Free Writing

Here I free write, as I did at the last OC Writer's write-in. Wonder what I will use. What I will post. Whether I will do a data drop and just publish this and other writing that I've done. Wonder whether anyone would enjoy reading this.

I prefer to craft my writing. Edit. Rewrite. Who knows? Maybe I can do a dump every once in a while to show people what I do at times.

***

This is, perhaps, how I think. Perhaps it provides some insight into how I think. Why anyone would care, I don't know.

I was tempted to go back and read and edit what I'd written, then thought better of it. Free writing is free writing. Just let it flow. Just go with the flow.

How often do I write like this? Not often enough. But I do have bits and pieces of unused writing on my computer and in journals.

Years ago, threw out a chest full of my writing. Mistake. Will not do again.

***

Just finished my seltzer water. Refreshing. Have a headache. Maybe the ice made it too cold. Maybe I'm anxious. Maybe both.

Shallow deep breath, kind of deep-ish breath, okay it wasn't deep at all, but I do need to relax. Instead, I shall work myself up into a... I don't want to type work myself up into a lather - just too lame. Work myself up into a tizzy - also lame. Is it okay to say lame? Politically incorrect.

Not what you want to do when you free write. Don't want to let word choice or political correctness get in the way of writing. Just write.

Poetry Reading in Long Beach

Sunday, I drove up to Long Beach for the *On The Edge* poetry reading of Ra Avis, Bill Friday, and Matthew Blashill. I was nervous about going to a poetry reading, as I haven't attended artsy hip anything in decades. As I drove through downtown Long Beach, I felt very suburban middle-aged.

Once there, though, I was made to feel welcome. Turns out I wasn't the only middle-aged attendee, nor was I the only attendee who lived in South Orange County. Nice to meet people in person who you have read and interacted with online.

Suffering from fried brain right now. Have accidentally published drafts of this post at least twice. Sorry to those completely confused, wondering, "Where the hell did that post go?" I probably should have left well enough alone and simply edited the piece. Brief, but done. At least for now.

***

Toast for Breakfast, Toast for Lunch

I remember when I was seven years old, the day I turned seven. We (my sister and I) were staying at the Hans Brinker Inn in the Netherlands as our parents enjoyed two weeks in Paris.

I was furious with my parents for having abandoned us for those two weeks. At Hans Brinker, every meal consisted of toast - toast with sugar and cinnamon for breakfast, toast with cheese or tomato for lunch, for dinner, I don't recall.

But that day, the day of my seventh birthday, we were eating our lunch of toast, and our parents came to pick us up. My sister, who was only four at the time, ran up to our parents. I, on the other hand, held them responsible. I was incensed.

The owner had pushed me down the stairs. They separated me and my sister into different rooms. She didn't understand. Her roommates didn't speak English. I was punished for going to her when she cried. I begged for them to put us in the same room.

So, I ignored my parents. Seething, I kept my back to them. They thought I didn't want to leave.

***

Verbal, Non-Verbal

Sometimes, I'm verbal

The words rush

They press

They insist on getting out of my head

They keep me awake at night

Unless I shut them up

Turn them off with meds

Sometimes, though,

I'm simply not

Sometimes, I'm non-verbal

The words are not there

I do jigsaw puzzles

Watch TV

Play with numbers

Rather than words

When the words fly

They are raucous

Noisily filling my mind

Needing to get out

I need relief

So, I write

Then, I must get

The racing commentary

Out of my mind

Onto the screen or paper

In black and white

Where later I reshape them

Edit them into something coherent

Perhaps

Or, perhaps,

Sometimes, I leave them

In a jumbled mess

All over the page

Mind Spinning

Let Me Off This Ride!

Mind spinning

In circles

Like a hamster

Or a wheel

Racing

Round and round

Going nowhere

Going nowhere

Too quickly

To safely

Get off

Mind spinning

Sick to my stomach

Let me off

This ride

Right now

Please slow down

Please brake

Cannot take it

Anymore

Maybe I shouldn't

Have had

Two cups of

Coffee

This morning

***

Dancing to White Noise

Within the white noise of the fan, she heard music and she danced. Her
mind arranged the notes. Her body responded. Music and dance made

serse. White noise, not so much.

The white noise bombarded her senses. too many notes. She picked out those that felt beautiful, that made sense to her. Her mind found and arranged the notes to quiet the noise.

The music was so soft, the volume so low, it faintly played in the background of the senseless cacophony of white noise. When she turned off the fan, the music was gone. Her room quiet. She no longer danced.

***

Barely Fiction: Kate.1

Her true and legal name is Kitt Kathleen O'Malley. She loves her name and is grateful her parents came up with it, a great stage name if there ever was one. Her first name is typically a nickname for Katherine or Kathleen, so her name is redundant.

She had thought that Katherine meant catharsis, or purification through emotional release, a meaning she's always identified with. Now that she researches her name, the etymology is unclear, perhaps originating with the goddess Hecate, who was capable of both good and evil, perhaps a metaphor for bipolar diagnosis.

Anyway, yes, she openly expresses strong emotions, perhaps less so now that she's medicated for bipolar disorder. She remains theatrical, loving attention and being on stage. She's also a Leo, so add that to the mixture.

For this piece of flash fiction, she'll go by Kate. Why? Because she named this piece Kate before she started writing and because it ties into the "Kiss me, Kate?" poem which ensues. Is she a shrew, a woman of violent temper and speech? At times she has been, but she hasn't overthrown a table in over a year or two (she just did that once). She has been known to throw adult temper tantrums. Something she's not proud of. Luckily her meds and psychotherapy help her keep an even keel.

***

Kiss me, Kate?

Good luck

You cannot tame this shrew

This woman of sometimes

Violent temper and speech

She remains wild and free

At heart a non-conformist

Pugnacious and proud

***

Writing in third person, as true or as outlandish as she pleases, taking lib-

186

erties with the facts, perhaps this will grow into an autobiographical novel. More likely than not, these words will remain here as a flash and then die the death of so many other blog posts, lost over a relatively short time period to the archives.

***

Barely Fiction: Kate.2

In the early '60s, on a pleasant August morning in San Francisco, Kate entered this world as the first daughter of her parents, Brandan and Ruby O'Brien, both firstborns in their respective families. They, all three of them, were members of the firstborn club, the club of overachievers, of type A personalities. Three type A's in a four-person family, perhaps a bit much for that fourth person, Kate's younger s ster (affectionately still thought of as her "baby" sister).

After Kate was born, Ruby stopped working in public relations and personnel at McCormick-Shilling to stay home with her daughter. Brandan worked for Standard Oil as a chemical engineer. When Kate was two, her father had an opportunity to move to Saudi Arabia to work for Aramco (then Arabian American Oil Company, now Saudi Aramco or Saudi Arabian Oi Company). The three O'Briens moved to Saudi Arabia, where Kate lived for five years, from ages two to seven.

When Kate was almost three, her mother Ruby gave her a baby sister. Yep. That baby was hers. Kate considered the baby the best birthday present ever. Her sister was far superior to any of Kate's lifeless, boring dolls. She moved of her own volition, cried, laughed, peed, and had her very own personality.

When Kate's mother Ruby was pregnant, and after she gave birth to her baby sister, Kate would inform everyone within listening distance that she had itsy-bitsy, teeny-weeny babies inside her and that once she grew up she'd go to the hospital and have them cut out, just like her mom did. Clearly, she didn't understand the fine points of reproduction or birth. She just reasoned that her sister grew inside her mom's belly until her mom had to the hospital to get her out. To her, going to the hospital meant getting surgery. How else would they get her sister out of her mother's belly?

About this time, Kate developed her skills as a surgeon by operating on her stuffed animals. She'd cut them open to remove unwanted parts (usually pesky noise-makers), and then would sew them back up. Perhaps she operated on her toys when she was older than three. Well, she knows that she did it when she lived in Dhahran. That much she remembers clearly.

As for that adorable baby sister, Ruby and Brandan considered naming the baby Jamila, which means beautiful in Arabic, for she was born in Saudi Arabia. Though they didn't name her Jamila, in this story she's named Jamie, with a nod to Jamila, as she was and still is quite beautiful. Kate will do her best to leave her far more private sister out of this story, except to boast from time to time. As a proud big sister, she has bragging rights. Plus, remember, this is fiction.

The O'Briens lived in modest 2-bedroom garden apartments within company compounds in Dhahran, Abqaiq, and Ras Tanura. Kate remembers going to the compound fence while her mother played tennis, looking out and seeing unending desert, and nomadic Bedouins traveling with their camel caravans.

Saudi Arabia was really hot and sandy. Kate doesn't miss extreme heat or sandstorms. To this day, she can't stand heat, be it dry or humid. She was made for foggy, boggy places, like the climates of her Irish and Germanic ancestors. In company compounds, they dressed as Americans did in the '60s. So, when Kate got stuck in a sandstorm, wearing a sleeveless mini-dress that left her face, arms and legs unprotected, the sand blinded her, and felt like millions of needles cutting into her exposed skin. Robes are functional in the desert. You need to cover your face, too, during a sandstorm.

Kate attended preschool, kindergarten, and first grade in Dhahran. In the private Dhahran American school within the compound, Kate had both Arab and American friends and classmates. They were taught an advanced American curriculum, plus the English-speakers learned Arabic (and the Arabic-speakers, English). Even though she did learn some Arabic in school, she no longer remembers it. To go to high school, kids had to go to boarding school outside the country, or their families moved. Many families moved, rather than send their teens to boarding schools.

What she misses most from her years in Saudi Arabia is Abdu, their Yemeni domestic worker. The term used in the mid-60s among Americans in Arabia was "house boy," clearly offensive. Abdu was not a boy. He was a dignified man, a husband and a father. Though everyone lived in modest apartments, everyone had help. The men lived in dormitories on the compound, and sent their earnings back home to their families.

Mr. and Mrs. O'Brien taught their daughters to show Abdu respect. They explained that he had a wife and a daughter Jamie's age back in Yemen and had come to Saudi Arabia to support his family, and save money to open a shop one day. Kate loved Abdu. When he babysat, he brought 6 oz bottles of Coca Cola and Juicy Fruit gum. He let them watch TV. Her favorite program was *Daktari,* about a veterinarian in East Africa. Kate loved the antics of the chimp named Judy and lion named Clarence.

Back in the '60s, most American Aramco employees and their spouses didn't bother to learn Arabic. Kate's parents did. When her mother was in the hospital having her sister removed (in labor), the Bedouins were fascinated by her mother, as she was the first white woman they had met. The nursing staff intervened and tried to separate them from her mother. Ruby refused to let the nurses keep them apart. She spoke to the Bedouin women in Arabic, for she was just as interested in them as they were in her.

Once, when Ruby brought Kate and Jamie to visit their grandparents in Seattle, she knew something was wrong with Brandon. She frantically called Aramco and demanded that she be told what was wrong with her husband. At that exact moment, there was a poisonous gas leak where Brandon was working. He didn't want any of his workers to climb the ladder to close the valve, for inhaling the gas stopped all body functions immediately. Brandan took a deep breath, climbed the ladder, closed the valve, but on his way down gasped, inhaled the gas and fell to the ground. He was not breathing, and his heart had stopped. His workers carried him to safety and resuscitated him. Kate's parents believed that the workers saved his life because he had taken the time to learn Arabic and speak to them in Arabic (plus he risked his life to save theirs).

Kate's proud of her parents. Both Brandan and Ruby are pretty kick ass.

***

Finished Scrivener Tutorial!

October 2015, I last modified the import of my blog into Scrivener thinking I'd massage my writing into a book. The next month, my mother had a stroke. Never got back to the book, or to figuring out Scrivener. Just finished the tutorial.

Enrolled in *National Association of Memoir Writers (namw.org)* online memoir writing course and will be attending the *Southern California Writers' Conference (writersconference.com)* later this month. The conference features memoir writing this year!

My first Scrivener project contains my outdated blog dump. Sometimes I edit old posts and pages, so I need to figure out how to import my current version of this site. Haven't had luck so far today. I did create a blank new project into which I plan to organize my writing under four categories:

- Kate -- fictionalized autobiography, starting at the beginning...

- Bipolar -- mental health focus

- Parenting My Son -- my son has struggled with migraines since he was two

- Parents with Dementia -- both my parents have dementia and live in memory care

Wish me luck. I may go nowhere with putting together and publishing my writing. At least I'm writing here. Actually, I'm pretty happy with blog writing.

***

Organizing in Scrivener

Right now, I'm writing in WordPress online. I write using whatever is handy, WordPress, Word, Google Docs, Pages on my iPad, emails to myself, even paper and journals (unfortunately, I cannot read my handwriting and I type faster).

When I first purchased Scrivener, I copied and pasted my blog posts from September 2013 to October 2014. Then I stopped, overwhelmed by the complexity of Scrivener. Now that I did the tutorial, I'm organizing those posts. Feels good. Really good.

Later I will add pieces written since then.

ADVOCATE

My purpose has grown over the years. What started out as self-help has grown to include helping others. While in seminary, the more papers I wrote, the more I realized that my calling was mental health advocacy, what would be called mental health ministry in the Christian tradition.

To be an advocate means to go from fighting for yourself and your own mental health to fighting for others, standing up to stigma, and voting for legislation that funds mental health treatment. For me it started with being honest and open. From there it grew through my writing, my online social media activity, and my involvement with the National Alliance on Mental Illness (NAMI.org).

Back in 2014, I wanted to volunteer for NAMI. To do so, I had to take NAMI's Peer-to-Peer class. As I found out, I had much to learn from the class. This, in spite of the fact that I have been a mental health consumer since I was eighteen years old, and in 1992 I was licensed as a Marriage and Family Therapist (then the license was called Marriage Family and Child Counselor).

NAMI Peer-to-Peer Recovery Education Program© introduced me to the concept of mental health recovery. The concept does NOT mean that those of us living with serious mental disorders will be cured or symptom free. The concept of recovery offers hope. Hope was what was missing in my life.

NAMI Peer-to-Peer taught me the BRIDGES (Building Recovery of Individual Dreams and Goals through Education and Support) Consumer Stages of Recovery, which I paraphrase here. That model starts with a crisis event, such as psychosis, suicide attempt, mania, or episodes of severe depression. The crisis requires recuperation, which is a stage of dependence After the trauma of a mental illness episode, we are exhausted -- body, mind and spirit.

After recuperation, comes time to decide to move forward. That decision must be made by those of us recovering from a crisis event. As we rebuild independence, we may need help to learn and practice living skills.

Finally, we experience an awakening. We realize that we are somebody with hopes and dreams. This is mental health recovery. We build healthy interdependence. Here we discover who we are and who we want to be, who we care about and who cares about us.

For many, this stage leads to advocacy. We accept ourselves, appreciate others, and grow confident. Now we channel our anger at injustice by taking assertive actions and helping others.

Now, just to be clear, blogging and NAMI volunteer work were not my first taste of advocacy. I've always been an outspoken rabble rouser and was politically active on campus and in my twenties. I've simply come full circle. My passions remain the same. My perspective has changed. I've lived it now. What I lack in youthful or unmedicated hypomanic energy, I make up for in wisdom, a lifetime of experience, and different perspectives – that of a consumer, mother, wife, daughter, and (former) psychotherapist.

***

Public Speaker in my Thoughts and Dreams

Imagine myself as a public speaker. Keep on seeing myself orating, speaking to others. I enjoy it. I am a narcissist. Besides, I've done it well. Two eulogies, one for each of my mother's parents, were my most satisfying speeches. Brought people to laughter and to tears. Won debates in junior high and high school. In junior high I convinced the class that aliens had visited the Earth. Drama geek in high school. Later in high school, as Scarlett O'Hara, I persuaded the class that slavery was moral, right, and necessary. Scary how easily people can be swayed. My ability to manipulate, to pull heartstrings, to seem to make sense, even when my arguments were not correct, scared me. Whether and how to use this gift, I wonder.

***

Social Media Here I Am

Down the rabbit hole of social media... At the end of last month, I set up social media accounts with multiple outlets, automatically publishing links to my WordPress blog articles and posting photos to Instagram, Google+ and Flickr.

In short, I'm feeling a little overwhelmed with having to keep up so many "windows" to my work. Anyway, social media, here I am.

Posting doesn't take my time and energy; liking and following others does. Once again, my energy is zapped when I stretch myself too thin. So many pictures, artwork, and thoughts, feelings and commentary to like and comment on. So many people out there in cyberspace. Will have to limit my activity at some point, probably sooner than later for my health and the health and well-being of my small family, who depend on me.

***

The Gathering on Mental Health and the Church

Last Friday I attended The Gathering on Mental Health and the Church at Saddleback Church. The all-day conference was a joint effort of Pastor Rick and Kay Warren of Saddleback Church, Bishop Kevin Vann of the Roman Catholic Diocese of Orange, and National Alliance on Mental Illness (NAMI) Orange County, as well as other faith and community leaders.

At the beginning of the day, I felt that I was in the perfect place, but as the day progressed, I grew weary, as well as leery. Weary, because it was a very long day with much to take in, much even for me who has lived it, practiced it, and studied it. Not only am I a mental health survivor, but I am a former mental health provider. Not only am I a child of God, but I have attended seminary. Furthermore, the content of my work in seminary, much of my writing, in particular my paper on Mental Health Ministry, dealt with this conference's focus.

Yet I pull back from organizational structure, from brick and mortar churches, from groups in general. I fear a loss of self, an inability to preserve my identity, to take care of myself. I fear becoming engulfed, subsuming my own needs and separateness from the needs of the whole. I fear drowning.

Perhaps I overstate my fear. Perhaps it is unfounded. Perhaps I am perfectly capable of working within an organizational structure.

Then again, perhaps that is not where I belong. Perhaps I work better as an outsider, as a member of smaller, more casual, groups. I shy away from "like-mindedness." I embrace difference, tolerance, variety.

***

NAMI Peer-to-Peer

To join a NAMI (National Alliance on Mental Illness) Peer-to-Peer group, or not to join a NAMI Peer-to-Peer group? That is the question. If I am to volunteer for NAMI, I must first participate in a NAMI Peer-to-Peer group. This makes sense, yet I fear it. Though I speak openly of having bipolar disorder, honestly, I distance myself from those sicker than I am. Shades of grey, I suppose. I am, or at least I appear to be, "high functioning." Few, if any, could tell from looking at me, or talking to me, that I have a mental illness. My appearance and behavior are socially acceptable and appropriate. No one can see what I think, or how I think, how quickly my mind races at times.

Recently I began attending a group of my psychiatrist's patients. This group I enjoy. We come with different presenting problems. Everyone is what could be described as "high functioning." I have a fear of peer-led support groups, and value a skilled, trained mental health professional as group leader. Peer groups serve an important function in recovery from mental illness, for people need a place to go for support, and many do not have the resources required to get the support they need from professionals. I guess my fear of peer-led groups goes back to my fear of losing myself in a group; it's a boundary issue. I need some structure, some "professional," impartial distance. I need an outsider to help me maintain my otherness.

***

Found Notes

Recently found some notes I jotted down while attending a workshop at The Gathering on Mental Health and the Church at Saddleback Church. Here they are:

1. Enjoy speaking to individuals and small groups.

2. Anxious when hear mental health professionals discussing mental health crisis intervention. PTSD for me. Difficult past experience. Do not want to go back there.

3. Anxious interacting with and seeing those more severely disturbed than I, those functioning less well with their illness. I, too, feel other. Other than the most disturbed.

4. Boundary issues: church groups, organizations of all types, employment workplaces, all threaten me with the risk of loss of self to the group.

5. Crisis intervention, hospitalization, peer-to-peer and family-to-family NAMI groups provoke fear in me. Once again, goes back to boundary issues. How do I protect myself, maintain some emotional distance? How to and whether I can say no?

6. Fiction writing? Fictionalizing personal experience? Once upon a time, in my late twenties, I had a boyfriend who was also a poet.

He recommended that instead of journal writing in first person, I should write in third person, fictionalize it, distance myself from it, be less self-absorbed and more creative.

7. Maybe now I participate in writers' groups and group therapy and later Toastmasters. That's all I want or can take on right now.

8. Do not, should not join/work for/volunteer for ANY organization, be it corporate or congregational.

OMG, just today on April 24th, I realized (or realized again, for this should not be news to me) that my fear of being engulfed by a group stems in part from family of origin dynamics. How many years of therapy have I had, anyway? Since age eighteen! I'm fifty now. AND, I once was a psychotherapist. Come on, Kitt. Get with it. Wake up. Grow up.

***

Overwhelmed by Social Media

I am quickly becoming overwhelmed by the time and attention-sucking nature of maintaining a broad social media presence.

***

MFT License Activated

Just completed the continuing education units (CEU) required to renew and reactivate my California Marriage and Family Therapist license (LMFT) and sent my license renewal to the California Board of Behavioral Sciences. In discerning whether to do so, I had this email exchange with my friend CJ:

KO: Right now, I am looking into taking CE to renew my MFT license as active. I've had an inactive license since they offered such a thing. Yes, I have maintained my license for twenty years without practicing psychotherapy because I put lots of work, many internship hours, graduate school debt, and written and oral exam prep into it. Blood, sweat, and tears (actually, the tears were on behalf of a least a couple of my clients whom I loved and who suffered greatly). What do you think of me activating my license, not necessarily putting out a shingle, at least not a brick and mortar shingle, and not now for money?

CJ: I still have my teaching certificate even though it would be a sad day if I ever return to the classroom. But since my plan is to live forever, I imagine sooner or later it will be useful. Don't let MFTing plans distract you if you've already found rhythm with life as it is. It seems you are generally a good gatekeeper to stuff that would lead to overwhelm. Does wanting you to place priority on clouds, bark, and flowers make me the worst career counselor ever? Yeah, probably so. But maybe not.

KO: Clouds, bark, tree roots and flowers take precedence without doubt. In my blogging and social media activity, I find myself counseling fellow mental health consumers. I have no desire to make a living at it, but am finding a voice. The voice has been as a mental health consumer and former psychotherapist. Now perhaps it is as a consumer and licensed psychotherapist who volunteers her advice via her blog persona. Although the Internet allows for a worldwide reach, the scope of any psychotherapy practice I undertake is limited by my license to the state of California. I have no intention to set up shop in the real world any time soon. Who knows where I'm headed?

***

Where Am I Going from Here?

Went to group therapy Tuesday and attended my first Toastmasters meeting earlier that day. Toastmasters was very structured, probably too structured for my tastes, though worked well in that they covered a lot of ground in one hour. Mentioned in group that I completed my continuing education units to renew my Marriage and Family Therapist license on an active basis and got positive feedback. I was afraid that my psychiatrist would disapprove. Not sure why. Guess I don't yet feel competent enough, well enough; though that fear may be unfounded. I do, of course, have some catching up to do in terms of professional development, having been out of the loop for a couple of decades. This is the first time since I was thirty that I have seriously considered, and took steps toward re-entering the mental health field, as a licensed professional.

Where am I going from here? Well, for one thing, whether or not I attend Toastmasters again, I consider myself an orator to be, an orator at heart. I'm sure Toastmasters would be helpful, but I do not feel comfortable with the format. Time tested, yes, but, well, I don't know, maybe it's just that part of me that doesn't like dancing choreographed steps. I chafe at structure. I know, or so I've been told, that structure is helpful, necessary even, for those with bipolar disorder. But, I prefer to live my life with fewer constraints.

Princess to Queen

When in high school, I overheard a "friend" say as I approached, "Here comes our Princess." I was shocked to learn that this was how my friends saw me. Apparently, I was a Princess, and now I must be a Queen. Indeed, I was a drama geek, an actress. Apparently, I was also somewhat aloof. Finally, I lived in a big house on the beach. Once a few of my classmates referred to the girls who lived on The Strand as stuck-up bitches. I said, "I live on The Strand." They responded, "Not you, Kitt." Honestly, in many ways I hated that house. But, this post isn't about socioeconomic dividing lines. Here, I write about ego, my gaping maw of an ego, and its need to be stroked. My husband adores me, but I lack a fawning audience.

Someday I do believe I will return to the stage, to the podium, to the public. Who knows? It may be silly to call myself an aspiring public speaker, since I do not aspire to do so any time soon. I'm talking four years down the line. That is my goal. In the meantime, I go to group therapy and to writers' groups. Not even ready for Toastmasters. Not yet. Toastmasters might not be the right venue for me. It's time-tested, somehow it felt artificial, forced, and inorganic.

Oh, I just recalled my interim goal of talking to a webcam. Yes, that's right. That is on my To Do list. That damn To Do list. Wonder when I'll get around to setting myself in front of a webcam?

***

I'm Back

My California Marriage and Family Therapist license is now current and renewed until May 31, 2016. Inactive license no more. Yes, that's right, inactive no more. Coming out of a long, very long, two-decade long, sabbatical. Wahoo!

My original license date was July 1, 1992. I graduated with a master's in psychology from New College of California in June 1990, was an intern for two years, logged the required 3,000 internship hours, passed my written and oral exams, and received my original license. As an intern, and later as a licensed psychotherapist, I worked with battered women, severely emotionally disturbed (SED) latency-aged (pre-adolescent) children, pregnant and parenting teenagers, SED adolescent girls in residential treatment, and finally SED adolescent boys in day treatment, until I burned out and fell into a deep depression at the age of thirty. Since then I have not practiced psychotherapy professionally. My training has come in handy, of course, but it has not inoculated me from mental illness or the hardships of life.

It feels good to be back, to reclaim my professional training, to not think of myself as unable to do what I had worked so hard to achieve. Once again, I see myself as capable of helping others. And, it feels good, really good.

***

NAMI Peer-to-Peer

This past Wednesday I attended my first of 10 National Alliance for Mental Illness (NAMI) Peer-to-Peer sessions. Since I am brain dead after excessively tweeting (yes, I've been hypomanic), here is my tweet about it from Wednesday night: "Just got home from 1st NAMI Peer to Peer class. Weird after over thirty years of therapy, but hey 1st time for everything. Always learning."

I will blog about what it is like to participate in NAMI's highly structured, scripted program and how it differs from my experiences in individual and group psychotherapy. I'm a seasoned consumer of individual psychotherapy, but believe (and hope) that I will learn some hands-on skills from NAMI's Peer-to-Peer program. Who knows, once I have finished the sessions, perhaps I will do some volunteer work with NAMI.

***

Not My Last Advocate Post

This is far from my last advocate post. I haven't even gotten started We who live with mental illness must organize and speak up.

1.   We lack psychiatrists

2.   We lack psychiatric beds

3.   We lack good quality psychiatric care, both inpatient and outpatient

4.   Our mental health system is broken

5.   Mental health care workers, including psychiatrists, are over-

whelmed

6. Most psychiatrists refuse to accept Medicare, leaving those of us on disability without psychiatric care

7. Rural areas lack psychiatrists, psychotherapists, mental health support groups, and quality medical care in general

We with mental illness must organize and speak up! We are not alone.

***

Full Circle

This morning I interviewed with Mental Health Association of Orange County to be a volunteer Hearing Advocate representing clients placed on mental health holds (involuntary psychiatric hospitalization for 72-hours).

Tomorrow I start my training by shadowing an MHA advocate at Mission Hospital Laguna Beach Behavioral Health Services, where in February 2005, I spent two weeks *voluntarily* hospitalized. No doubt being taken to the hospital *involuntarily* is a quite different experience than going there *by choice.*

The rooms have incredible views of the Pacific, as the hospital sits on Pacific Coast Highway (PCH). As a voluntary patient, I appreciated the views, but was not permitted to walk to the beach until I left the hospital and entered the partial hospitalization program. After eating lunch, as outpatients we had the freedom to walk down to the beach, which we often did together as a group. Laguna Beach is truly beautiful. Unfortunately, you need quite a bit of money to live there (and traffic is horrible on PCH).

***

I Loved It! ~ Patients' Rights Advocacy

Loved shadowing an MHA Hearing Advocate earlier today. Look forward to learning more. Great opportunity for me to make use of my experience, having been psychiatrically hospitalized for bipolar disorder (albeit voluntarily), while dusting off old knowledge and skills from my education, and the careers of my early adulthood. After all, I have a bachelor's in legal studies, and experience as a legal assistant, a master's in psychology, and counseling skills gained as a Marriage and Family Therapist, and advocacy skills. Those careers date back to my twenties. I'm 51 as I write this. In between, I spent a decade working in commercial real estate and a decade on disability, sometimes struggling to do something as simple as make dinner.

Californians with mental illnesses who are receiving treatment in mental health facilities, including those persons subject to involuntary commitment, are guaranteed numerous rights under State and federal laws, including the right to be free from abuse and neglect, the right to privacy, dignity, and humane care, and the right to basic procedural protections in the commitment process.

***

Choices, Choices

Okay, so maybe this isn't the proper forum to be weighing pros and cons of volunteer opportunities. So far, I've shadowed two MHA Hearing Advocates to three different hospitals over two Fridays. Last Friday I was sick, and the Hearing Advocate I had hoped to shadow never called. I've been playing telephone tag with him.

The hospital in Laguna Beach, which is nearest my home, is the nicest. How many hospitals have ocean views? I do not know if the program is as good as it was a decade ago when I was admitted voluntarily inpatient for two weeks, and then in partial hospitalization for a few months. Then, the program was highly structured. Patients were not allowed to mill about and loiter. You were in actively participating group, or you were to stay in your room. At mealtimes and breaks, we could enjoy the break room, watch TV, and "walk the circuit." The ward rooms were arranged in a circle, enabling fluid movement, rather than unsettling and caged pacing.

I do not know the details of the programs at these three hospitals. I do know that I got "bad vibes" at the two I visited on my last shadow training. Patients seemed like they were wandering about without much structure. Perhaps it was too close to lunch time, but many of the patients seemed too ill to participate in structured group activities. My sense was (and I'm sensitive to these things) that at any time, someone could be set off and chaos would ensue. I didn't feel particularly safe, nor did I feel welcome.

There, I said it. I felt perceived by the more paranoid or aggressive patients as part of the system that "imprisoned" them. Honestly, I'm at a loss. These people were very sick and needed help. You do not want to release someone from the hospital when they are not ready, only for them to then go kill themselves or hurt someone else. The decisions Hearing Officers make is difficult. They must balance the right to freedom against the greater good.

When we are ill, we do not always think clearly, we do not always behave in our best interest, or in the best interest of the greater good. – Kitt O'Malley

So, now, my other option: Today I interviewed at NAMI. They have several volunteer opportunities I may enjoy, and for which I may be well suited. Among them: becoming a Peer-to-Peer mentor teaching the Peer-to-Peer class, becoming a In Our Own Voice speaker, volunteering at special events by sitting at their table, handing out information and answering questions, and even volunteering in their office. I would NOT be doing all these activities. Both the Peer-to-Peer mentor and In Our Own Voice speaking require training, which I greatly appreciate. I am impressed with NAMI's structured training programs. I NEED structure.

Perceived risk of chaos and danger trigger me. I do not need that in my life.

In writing this, I'm pretty sure I have made up my mind. I cannot handle being a Hearing Advocate right now. In fact, if truth be told, I respect people who are highly motivated to seek treatment, and am at a loss about how to best help those who do not want help, who do not see themselves as being helped by a medical model. I am 100 percent behind improving our mental health system, including making hospitals hospitable for patients, their visitors, their advocates, and mental health providers.

***

Ending the Silence

Today is the first day of 2015. I'm bundled under the covers in my bed typing on my laptop. My husband brought me cornflakes and coffee so he could watch *The Omen* downstairs in Spanish. I am a scaredy-cat and cannot watch movies with ominous (get it? *The Omen*, ominous) music tracks, even if I have no idea what's being said.

Just now I completed the Ending the Silence volunteer application for my local Orange County chapter of NAMI. Pretty in-depth application, so I thought I would share my answers with you.

LIST OTHER NAMI PROGRAMS YOU HAVE PARTICIPATED IN AND YOUR ROLE IN THE PROGRAM:

I participated in NAMI's Peer-to-Peer training as a peer participant or student. Although I have a master's in psychology, a Marriage and Family Therapist license, been in therapy since I was eighteen-years-old (over thirty years), have participated in group therapy ten years ago when hospitalized for two weeks and during months of partial hospitalization, I learned A LOT. I feared that I would feel out of place but did not. NAMI's Peer-to-Peer training is excellent and covers much information, perhaps too much information. I wanted to get my hands on the instructors' manuals so that I could go into greater depth. That's how impressed I was. The program introduced me to the concept of recovery vis-à-vis mental illness and gave me hope. HOPE!

DESCRIBE ANY BACKGROUND IN EDUCATION:

MA in psychology (1990) and LMFT (licensed in 1992, though I have not practiced in more than twenty years). When I practiced psychotherapy, I worked with severely emotionally disturbed (SED) elementary and middle school-aged children, pregnant and parenting teens, and severely emotionally disturbed (SED) adolescents in residential (level 14, which is the most restrictive private setting in California – one step from state hospitalization or California Youth Authority) and day-treatment. My son is fourteen. I have experience mothering him and volunteering in his elementary school classrooms.

Psychotherapist, 1990 – 1993

Individual, family, group, and milieu psychotherapy of severely emotionally disturbed adolescents in residential treatment program.

Counselor, 1990 – 1992

Counseled pregnant and parenting adolescents. Agency liaison to Young Mothers' Clinic at Kaiser Permanente Medical Center.

Field Placement, 1989 – 1990

Individual, family, and milieu psychotherapy of severely emotionally disturbed children in day treatment program.

Administrative Coordinator, 1988 – 1989

Non-profit administration of battered women's shelter and counseling center. Crisis intervention. On-call supervision of crisis line and shelter intake.

WHY DO YOU WANT TO BE AN ENDING THE SILENCE PRESENTER?

First, as a former high school drama geek, I love getting on stage and speaking in front of an audience. I have a passion for ending stigma surrounding mental illness, educating the public about mental illness, and offering compassion and support to those living with mental illness and their loved ones. Currently I exercise my passion and commitment by mental health blogging at KittOMalley.com and prolific social media advocacy, and psychoeducation on multiple platforms. I am a former psychotherapist. I have lived experience with mental illness, namely bipolar disorder.

ENDING THE SILENCE IS AN EDUCATIONAL PROGRAM. WE DO NOT GIVE ADVICE OR COUNSEL HIGH SCHOOL STUDENTS OR THEIR TEACHERS. CAN YOU REFRAIN FROM GIVING ADVICE OR SUGGESTIONS?

Honestly, I could use the practice saying no, as people often turn to me for advice and counsel, and it overwhelms me. That is why I no longer practice psychotherapy. If I ever did return to the profession, I would require distance and clearly delineated boundaries. The distance of being an educator or public speaker, rather than providing therapy or even giving casual advice, is protective of MY boundaries and enables those in need to get proper care, such as psychiatric care, hospitalization, or psychotherapy.

WHAT DOES RECOVERY MEAN TO YOU?

Recovery is a relatively new concept for me, believe it or not. I always thought of it in terms of substance abuse. But NAMI's Peer-to-Peer course and my involvement in the mental health blogging community this past year and a quarter has opened my eyes to the concept of HOPE. When I first learned that I had bipolar disorder, and not depression, I was devastated. I had internalized shame and stigma attached to that diagnosis. I thought that the only direction my life and my mental health would take was a downward spiral. Not so. Although I must be mindful of my symptoms and adjust my lifestyle to suit my needs, I am still a productive member of society. There are ways of contributing aside from earning an income and climbing some preconceived ladder of success.

For me, recovery means overcoming my own internalized stigma and having hope that I can live well. I can live my life well even though I have a mental illness. I do contribute to society, even if I do not earn a handsome salary. I am of value. Recovering means learning how to best live with bipolar disorder.

Recovery means Hope for Now, and Hope for the Future.

WHAT ARE YOUR VIEWS ON TREATMENT (TRADITIONAL AND/OR NON-TRADITIONAL)?

I struggled with the symptoms of depression and cyclical overwork, leading to burnout and breakdown for twelve years before turning to a medical doctor for help. In those twelve years, I struggled with my symptoms using psychotherapy. Psychotherapy helped at times, for example, cognit ve restructuring rescued me from the precipice of suicide when I was 18. Perhaps at other times, it contributed to my depression, digging me in deeper and deeper without a clear way out. Medication, in conjunction with psychotherapy, helped with my depression, but it wasn't until I received the diagnosis of bipolar disorder that both my hypomania and my depression were acknowledged and treated properly. I support the use of medication, psychotherapy, and peer support.

I believe in taking care of your body, for the brain is influenced by exercise, sun, nutrition, vitamin D, and omega fatty acids. I believe in nontraditional treatments, such as aromatherapy, as adjuncts to medical treatment. Any nontraditional treatments should be shared with one's prescribing doctor, for herbal remedies and nutritional supplements are chemicals, too, and can either help or interfere with treatment. I take fish oil, vitamin D, try to exercise regularly, and like the soothing scent of lavender. My son finds that fresh lavender helps him when he is stressed or feeling the symptoms of a migraine coming. [I forgot to mention in my application the usefulness of mindfulness and prayer.]

***

Through the Lens of Our Past

When I was thirteen, my family went on vacation to Kauai. On that trip, men whistled at me. I thought they were perverts, whistling at a 13-year-old girl. Years later, looking at pictures from that trip, my father pointed to a photo of me and insisted that it was my mother, arguing that she had my mother's legs. I countered that I inherited my legs from my mom. Thanks, Mom, for the long legs. Maybe a tall, leggy 13-year-old looks more like a woman than a girl.

Later as a high school student, I wore my hair in a bun and brought a textbook or play to study while sunning on the beach. I thought I looked under-age, but I probably resembled a college student. When men approached me and said hello, I would curtly inform them I was jailbait and to go away. My husband believes that he spoke to me once when he was a college student. He recalls me giving him the brush off and pointing to my father to make my point and scare him away. He even remembers my father wearing his distinctive straw hat as he sat on our second-story deck overlooking the beach.

Flash forward a few decades: As a middle-aged mother of a 13-year-old boy, I was shocked at how physically mature his female classmates were. They *appeared* physically mature. Those girls *looked* like women, even though they most certainly were not. This is where laws, morality, social taboo, reason, and impulse control come in. As adults, we must protect those who may *LOOK* ready for what they are *NOT* yet ready. This is where the village – society – comes in. We must STOP and PUNISH those who take advantage of those younger and less mature.

I realize many adolescents are sexually active. Over twenty years ago, I counseled pregnant and parenting teens and provided psychotherapy to adolescents in residential treatment. Based on my experience as a clinician, the younger an adolescent becomes sexually active and the greater the disparity in age between sexual partners, the greater the imbalance of power in the relationship, the more abusive the relationship, and the more likely that the younger partner had been previously sexually abused.

***

Date Rape is Rape

Twice in one year, her senior year at UC Berkeley, she was raped by men she knew.

***

The first man was a friend of a couple of her housemates. He wanted her and pursued her relentlessly. She finally acquiesced to a date. After dinner at his place, he refused to take her home when she said she wanted to leave. He insisted she stay the night. She did not have taxi fare to leave and go home, so she submitted and stayed the night.

The word "submitted" sounded so wrong to her as a feminist, but it is how she felt. The feeling was alien and unnatural for her and caused her great shame. She thought of herself as strong and assertive, not as submissive.

The fact was she didn't feel safe alone on the streets of Oakland. She wasn't familiar with his neighborhood and had no idea how to get back to her own neighborhood near the Ashby BART station. Although it wasn't safe to travel by bus that late at night, it certainly wasn't safe staying. The whole experience disgusted her. She felt dirty and ashamed.

He would continue to call her, persistently hunting her, asking her out again and again. When he came over to visit her housemates, she would go upstairs to her bedroom. She avoided him. Just the thought of him made her physically ill.

***

The second date rapist was her former first love. She loved this young man. They remained friends, kept in touch over the years since they broke up, socialized with each other during winter and summer breaks and corresponded regularly their senior years thousands of miles apart.

He invited her to his senior prom at the prestigious Ivy League school he attended. She agreed to go with the explicit understanding that she would not be staying with him, and that they would not have sex. She made him promise to arrange accommodations to stay with female friends of his. He did not.

She arrived late at night. Once they got to his dorm, she asked where she was staying. He hadn't kept his end of the bargain. Again, she didn't feel like she had options.

They argued the evening of the prom, which they did not attend, instead they attended some apparently prestigious party. He flew her out to play the part of smart, beautiful, rich lover. He asked that she not mention that he paid the airfare. She was furious with him. At one point in the evening, she stormed out of the party, furious with him. Outside on the campus grounds, he broke down crying and dared to ask her for help. She shouted at him, not caring that others stared at them: "Are you kidding me? You raped me last night! Yes, you need help, but not from me. Helping you hurts me. So, no, I will not help you. It is not my job to teach you how to feel, how to understand the feelings of others. That is your job. You need help. Get professional help, not my help."

Legal Disclaimer: All characters appearing in this work are fictitious. Any resemblance to real persons, living or dead, is purely coincidental.

***

Stuck to the Couch

Another brief update as I'm taking it easy, trying to get myself over yet another bout of gastroenteritis. (I do not suffer nearly as much as my son does, but it has me struck me down, glued to the couch, not wanting to stand or make any sudden movements.) Anyway, this upcoming weekend I am training with NAMI to become a Provider Educator, that is one of their panel members who teach mental health providers what it is like to live with a mental illness or be a family member of someone living with a mental illness.

***

Been Busy

Friday: Attended NAMI Advocacy Training.

Saturday: Prepared parents' income tax return.

Sunday: Finished our income tax return.

No wonder I'm exhausted! Friday, I attended a NAMI California Regional Meeting in which we participated in NAMI Smarts for Advocacy Training. We learned how to turn our story of lived experience with mental illness into a two-minute pitch to ASK for specific change, such as voting for or against a piece of legislation, on behalf of those of us with lived mental health experiences.

***

Opportunity Knocks?

Yesterday I was volunteering at my local mental health nonprofit, which shall remain unnamed for now (okay, it was NAMI Orange County) I learned that one of their staff members recently gave their resignation. When they do list the position to be filled, I very well may apply for it.

No doubt many others will apply as well. Many with recent nonprofit administrative experience. Others who are very involved with NAMI OC as volunteers. The competition will be fierce.

Yet, it intrigues me. My local NAMI knows me. They know that I have bipo ar disorder. They know some of my skills. I like the office staff. We get alcng. Who knows? Maybe it will be a good fit for me.

Back in February 2014, I had considered returning to the workplace through the Social Security Ticket to Work program and was helped by YourEmploymentNetwork.com. Today I reestablished contact online, but I'm only interested in this one job. I do not know how that focus will work in terms of using Ticket to Work. I shall find out in due time.

If I do not get the job, then so be it. I just don't want to throw myself into the job market whole hog. I want to wait for and apply only for those jobs that align with my passion for mental health advocacy.

***

Thursday, I Did A Lot

Thursday, I did a lot. Much more than I would usually do. Much more outsice our home. Off the couch. In the community. Among colleagues and friends. What did I do, you wonder? Well, to start with, I volunteered from 9:30 am to 2:30 pm at my local NAMI Orange County.

I assisted their Educational Programs Coordinator by making phone calls and sending emails to register participants in an upcoming Provider Education course. Come January 2016, I will be teaching a Provider Education course for the first time. Both looking forward to it and feel a bit nervous.

While at NAMI, I spoke to their Volunteer Coordinator about helping with social media and marketing in preparation for the October NAMIWalks for Orange County. As the time approaches, I'll be begging folks to sponsor me.

Now, instead of applying for a paid job at NAMI, I offered to volunteer two days a week. That way, I'd ease myself back into the world outside my house and off my couch. Since my husband works and I receive disability, I do not need to work full-time, and quite frankly, social stimulation triggers hypomania and subsequent exhaustion in me.

After volunteering during the day, I had enough time to come home and quickly check my email, Twitter, and Facebook notifications. Then I was off to a fundraising event for a friend of mine who has survived breast cancer.

***

I'm Back and I'm Exhausted

I'm back from NAMI California's annual conference, held this year in Newport Beach (an easy commute from my home). Now I'm lying in bed completely exhausted. Met lots of great people. Younger adults and people of color underrepresented, unfortunately. I was one of the many older (mature) white folk in attendance. I alternated between volunteering at tables for the conference and attending presentations.

Got a chance to meet the colorful and creative Emily Wu Truong, who was wearing mental health awareness lime green. She's a sweetheart with a strong commitment to reaching out to young adults and the Asian community. Plus, she posted TONS of pics of folks at the conference on Facebook.

When I felt exhausted on Sunday, I visited the Welcome Center NAMI California had set up and drew a doodle.

Tomorrow I'll write more about some of the presentations I attended. Or, perhaps I'll get around to it next week, or who knows…never? (more likely tomorrow or next week)

***

Timely Psychology Coursework

Just completed these three timely and emotionally charged courses: Older Adults and Mental Health, School Refusal, and Chronic Illness in Children.

Yes, I'm firmly in the Sandwich Generation, parenting a sensitive adolescent, while caring for aging parents. Here I am in the middle, somehow balancing it all, even though I have bipolar disorder. I can hardly believe that I'm stable, all things considered.

I use my knowledge and skills parenting my son (which I do imperfectly), caring for my parents (also trial and error), and loving my husband.

***

Do We Have the Right to Die?

Though I preach hope and advocate that people try treatment instead of taking their lives, I wonder whether it is reasonable to decide to die when the pain is too great to bear and does not respond to any treatment.

I often feel disingenuous telling people that there is hope, for that is not always true. Some of us living with mental illness respond more effectively to medication, psychotherapy, support, exercise, good nutrition, meditation and so on. Some do not.

No one chooses to have "treatment resistant" mental illness. We cannot will mental illness away. Treatment does not always work. Still, sometimes there are options we have not considered, options supported by science, that just may work.

My friend Dyane Harwood chose ECT when medication failed her. ECT saved her life when she suffered deep bipolar depression. With the help of an astute psychiatrist, she eventually found that adding an "old school" MAOI to her medication mix helped.

I assume I will get some fire, and perhaps some concern, for this post.

FURTHER THOUGHTS ON THE ISSUE…

A first-of-its-kind report offers insights into the characteristics and outcomes of requests for euthanasia on the grounds of suffering related to psychiatric illness in Belgium, where it is legal.

'We found that when considering patients' demands seriously, most do find a way to continue with their life," Dr Thienpont said.

Thienpont, L. (2015). Euthanasia requests, procedures and outcomes for 100 Belgian patients suffering from psychiatric disorders: a retrospective, descriptive study. *BMJ Open, 5*(7), e007454. doi:10.1136/bmjopen-2014-007454.

Gallant, A. (2015). People With Mental Illness Deserve To Die With Dignity Too. *Huffington Post.* Retrieved from http://www.huffingtonpost.ca/arthur-gallant/mental-illness-suicide-_b_6637866.html

Melville, N. (2015). Assisted Suicide for Mental Illness Gaining Ground. *Medscape.* Retrieved from http://www.medscape.com/viewarticle/848910

***

Conferences This Summer

In August, I will attend (or at least I registered for and paid to attend) two conferences: BlogHer16: Experts Among Us in Los Angeles, and NAMI California: Back to the Future - Building on the Past for a Better Tomorrow in Burlingame, a suburb of San Francisco near SFO airport.

I'm kind of freaking out, worried about going to the conferences, nervous that I may become overwhelmed and trigger mood cycling (live in too much fear of triggering symptoms). I plan to stay in hotel rooms by myself, which will enable me to recuperate each day, and will give me somewhere to hide and decompress.

***

As part of BlogHer16, I joined the BlogHer Social Media Influencer Network, enrolling four of my social media channels for potential advertising: Facebook (personal profile), Facebook Fan Page, Twitter, and Instagram. This site will remain ad-free (for now).

Using my social media presences to advertise is a completely new thing for me. The ads will be clearly labeled as such (as is legally required). Honestly, not sure how comfortable I feel about it. Testing the waters.

***

NAMI Provider Education

Last month I enjoyed teaching NAMI's Provider Education course along with four other great panelists. This time I presented as an individual with mental illness. Last year I presented as a licensed mental health professional (no longer in practice) with lived experience of mental illness. Scheduled to do so again in mid-February.

CARETAKE

Consider caretaking advocacy in action. Let me explain. Not only do I support others in the mental health community, not only do I fight stigma, not only do I argue for better mental health funding and better quality of mental health care for the general public, I do so for my family, for those I love.

I am not only someone who has bipolar disorder, I am a mother, a wife, and a daughter. I am more than my diagnosis and must deal with more than my diagnosis. I have a family that needs me, that needs my help. Here I share my writing about caring for my migraineur son, who has struggled with depression and social anxiety, and overseeing the care of my parents.

Caring for a child with chronic illness, chronic pain, and mental health diagnoses is extremely difficult. You feel responsible. Mothers are often blamed for children's mental illnesses. Even though I'm committed to be the best mother I can be, I couldn't help but feel responsible in some way. To top that, I feel deep compassion for the pain my son has lived with his entire life.

Over the years, I've taken my son to numerous specialists and will continue to do so. Now that he's eighteen, he's an adult and bears responsibility in seeing to his health. Still, I fight for him as I encourage him to develop the skills needed to fight for himself.

In 2015, my mother had a major stroke leading to vascular dementia, putting me in the position of overseeing both hers and my father's care, for he already suffered from dementia. My mother's stroke was a huge blow to the family. My writing focused on the effects that tragedy had on her, on me, and on the family.

In writing about my parents and about my relationship with my son, I touch on the multi-generational aspect of brain disorders and family dynamics. Mental illness never involves just one person. Both genes and behavior patterns are passed down.

Many of us living with mental illness or brain disorder have co-morbid (co-occurring) chronic illnesses. Often, we are not treated for our "physical" illnesses, as many doctors dismiss them as psychosomatic. "Mental" illnesses ARE "physical" illnesses, and "physical" illnesses affect our "mental" illnesses. We are not just our brains, just our bodies, just our minds, just our feelings, or just our souls. The more we learn, the more we understand interconnectedness and comorbidities.

As an example of co-morbidity, in the Spring 2015 issue of the *Journal of Neuropsychiatry and Clinical Neurosciences*, researchers proposed The AL-PIM Spectrum. ALPIM stands for:

A = Anxiety disorder (mostly panic disorder);

L = Ligamentous laxity (joint hypermobility syndrome, scoliosis, double-jointedness, mitral valve prolapse, easy bruising);

P = Pain (fibromyalgia, migraine and chronic daily headache, irritable bowel syndrome, prostatitis/cystitis);

I = Immune disorders (hypothyroidism, asthma, nasal allergies, chronic fatigue syndrome); and

M = Mood disorders (major depression, Bipolar II and Bipolar III disorder, tachyphylaxis. Two thirds of patients in the study with mood disorder had diagnosable bipolar disorder and most of those patients had lost response to antidepressants).

"We conclude that patients with ALPIM syndrome possess a probable genetic propensity that underlies a biological diathesis for the development of the spectrum of disorders. Viewing patients as sharing a psychological propensity toward somatizing behavior essentially denies patients access to care for the diagnosable medical conditions with which they present."

– *J Neuropsychiatry Clin Neurosci.* 2015 Spring; 27(2):93-103. doi: 10.1176/ appi.neuropsych.14060132

***

The Window

Years ago, my father-in-law made this gorgeous stained-glass window to fit a port-hole window in our house. We've moved a few times since, with that window boxed up and stored for later resurrection. This past August, I decided it was time to frame and hang it. I ordered a custom frame from Northern Hardwood Frames, a Minneapolis, Minnesota custom stained-glass frame shop. Perfect, I thought, since my father-in-law met his wife, married, and started their family in Minnesota.

When visiting my in-laws in early September, I told him about the window and the frame I had ordered. He mentioned that he was thinking of selling his glass and supplies. I jumped at the chance to carry on his craft and bought a bunch of gorgeous glass he had collected over the years.

When the frame I had ordered arrived, my father-in-law was in the inten-
sive care unit fighting sepsis. I pulled out the window, hoping to frame and
hang it for my husband, but a piece was broken, and the lead stretched.
The window was a metaphor for my father-in-law's state. Still beautiful,
but needing repair. Fragile. Life and health, like this stunning window, are
fragile. As I love and pray for my father-in-law, I cherish his window and
look forward to someday repairing it, framing it, and hanging it in a place
of honor in our home. It represents, for me, the beauty, vibrancy and creativity of my father-in-law, the love he freely and generously gave, and the
love he inspires.

***

Balancing Priorities

Motherhood is difficult. Over the years, I have felt torn between mothering, being a devoted wife, working outside my home, studying in seminary,
and volunteering in my community. I have found myself repeatedly taking
on, and then reneging commitments due to conflicts in my responsibilites,
the primary one being motherhood. On top of it all, I struggle with a potentially debilitating mental illness, bipolar disorder. For now, I stay home and
write. Dust settles on and under furniture and the laundry waits.

***

Playing Therapist

At group this week, I played therapist. I was a PATIENT, not the therapist,
who, by the way, calmly and ably led the group. For a while, I took over. I
could not contain my reaction to what I heard. The part of me that reacts
to perceived danger and is impassioned about protecting people from vi-

olence could not stay calm. I had to put in my two cents. I always have to state my opinion. There I was, once again getting all worked up, REACTING, not sitting back and letting others come to their own conclusions.

Earlier that same day, I played therapist with someone who knows that I have bipolar disorder, that I blog about my mental illness, and that I once was a psychotherapist.

Part of this behavior of mine is symptomatic, part personality, part professional training, part vocational, part a calling. When I was in my twenties, I was a psychotherapist, a Marriage, Family and Child Counselor (MFCC). Now the license is called a Licensed Marriage and Family Therapist (LMFT). The former license name better described what I did, for most of my work was with adolescent girls. I maintain my license on an inactive basis, for I worked hard to get it, and I haven't quite closed the door on someday reactivating it and doing something with it. What that something is, I do not know. My vulnerability, my permeable boundaries, make me empathic and perceptive, but also put me at risk.

As a psychotherapist, I was not calm and reassuring. No, I did crisis intervention and broke down denial. I worked best with adolescent girls, who appreciate someone who is real, who shows their true self. I was a better case manager, professional nag, than impassive listener.

***

Mother and Wife

When my son was young, I juggled working outside the home with mothering and homemaking. By the time he was four, I found it unsustainable and ended up in a psychiatric hospital for two weeks and then months in partial hospitalization spending my days in structured group therapy sessions. Since then, I have been a full-time stay-at-home mother and wife, sometimes too overwhelmed to cook dinner.

Indeed, I was, and still am, too tired and overwhelmed to cook, but the cleaning, or lack thereof, is partly a resistance on my part. Let's face it, I hate housekeeping. I'm able to keep the house clean, but I hate doing so. My asthma and eczema get in the way, but even more so my intellect and proud stubborn nature do. I do not want to be a housekeeper. Mother, yes. Maid, no.

My greatest concern, my highest priority, is to be a good mother to my son. But a good housekeeper, nope. Neither job, motherhood, or housekeeping, requires intellect. Neither garners much in the way of positive feedback from others. Should I dust, vacuum, or do the laundry, my husband will notice and thank me. He is a decent guy. But, I never imagined I would be a stay-at-home mother. I always saw myself as a working professional with a nanny for child-care and maid-service to keep the cust bunnies at bay.

What happens when a once bright and promising student and professional is unable to maintain stability, to hold down an outside job while adequately parenting her child? The once straight-A student is now frustrated. I did attend seminary after my hospitalization, but as my diagnosis might predict, quit twice. First when we moved to Oregon, which destabilized and depressed me (seasonal affective disorder, too, great!), and a few years later when my husband was laid off during the recession, once again a destabilizing event.

Honestly, when I first realized that I was not "just" depressed (dysthymic), but was experiencing the symptoms of bipolar disorder, of mania, and got the medical help I needed for that more serious diagnosis, I put my son into full-time childcare because I didn't think that he was safe around me; I thought he'd be better off parented by someone else. It pains me to think about now.

So far, I haven't said much about being a wife. It's easier to write about being a mother. Not so sure how, or whether, to write about being a wife. I am thankful for my husband. I have not always been grateful for him. Marriage is not always easy. He is loving and supportive, and a great dad to our son.

***

Exhausted

Starting to recuperate from the last two weeks. Still exhausted. Sleepless nights, partly due to hypomania and stress, partly to dogs whining to go out in the wee hours of the morning. Too much 24/7 parenting. Home with my son almost two weeks, first when he had the stomach flu, second for spring break. Easter played a role; spending time with family can be double-edged. Love them, and they me. But it can be exhausting, over-stimulating, and, well, stressful, worrisome. Seeing my father's memory erode is painful. Seeing my mother's lymphoma tumor grow, scary. She is a fighter. With the help of cutting-edge cancer treatment, most notably monoclonal antibody therapy Rituxan, she has managed to keep her lymphoma at bay for thirty years. But this tumor is stubborn and will not go away. It is slow-growing, but still there. Please pray for her, as well as my father. Such is life in the sandwich generation, caring for a child while worrying about the health and well-being of aging parents.

***

Regrets

REGRET NOT BEING A GOOD ENOUGH MOTHER

Feeling sick, difficult to sit with how I have parented my son. It's been hard, but I have done my best. I feel sorry for him. He complains that I yell at him, that I am abusive, too loud. That he experiences me as abusive kills me, causes me great pain. I've tried SO HARD to be the best mother I could be. It has been SO IMPORTANT to me. And I've failed? How could this be? I know I have bipolar disorder. I know I have a temper. But abusive? I want to be a good mother, a good enough mother. It pains me to think that I may not be. His complaints may be unrelated to my diagnosis, save for the temper my son engages. My son and I push each other's buttons. We both pick and engage in fights with each other. Resentment builds on both sides, me wanting more freedom, him wanting more of me, of my attention. How much more can I give? I believe it is time to give less, not more. I've worked so very hard, for so very long. Please, God, help me be a good mother. Please, God, please.

REGRET LASHING OUT AT THOSE I LOVE

Remembering an old home movie of my mother as a girl, she danced circles around a group of family members standing on the sidewalk. They stood still. She couldn't. There was no music, yet she danced. That dancing girl, she is I, I am she. I am the girl dancing around the group, out of sync, dancing to my own music. There are other ways in which I resemble my mother. We share an ability to slay with words. She was not only the dancing girl, but the debate team captain. This characteristic, the pugilist in me,

I must restrain. I have been mean. I have lashed out at those I love. Please, God, help me be a kinder, more loving person.

REGRET WITHHOLDING LOVE

Recently my husband mentioned that he always says, "I love you" first and that I then respond, "I love you, too." Am I withholding love? Since he pointed out this dynamic to me, I've been saying "I love you" first more often.

Back in high school, a history teacher told me that I held people at a distance. At the same time, he said I was a people-person and should go into business, not medicine (I aspired to become a neurosurgeon). Which was it, aloof or social? Years later, when I was a legal assistant, I had a co-worker who claimed he didn't like me until he got to know me. He said I came off as a bitch at first. Some people don't like me because I act too smart and seem condescending. Maybe I protect myself by holding back, by putting on airs, by not participating, by hiding my flame, by covering my heart.

My goal is not to be liked. At the same time, I do not want to hurt people, least of all my husband and son. Please, God, help me give love freely without withholding.

***

Chafing at Structure?

The structure of my life: up at 7:00am; fix breakfast and lunch for my son; take him to school; the day is mine spent doing errands, going to writers' groups, occasionally writing, and maintaining my social media presence;

then pick son up from school; spend time with him after school, often shuttling him to and from and up and down the hills he loves to downhill mountain bike; fix dinner; and finally, relax with my husband and son in front of the TV. At the beck and call of our dogs, who want outside, then inside, then outside, then inside (bought a dog door, but need to install it); the overly excited labradoodle and standard poodle even accompany me in the car to and from my son's school. I know I should walk them twice a day, but since they recently chased a golden retriever while on leash and dragged me along the sidewalk, I'm not taking them out. They need the exercise, as do I. But I also need peace. I paid for dog training, but haven't yet started, just spoke over the phone with the trainer about their behavior.

This summer I will be home with my son full-time. Not sure how that will go. Like most of the stay-at-home moms I know, I always dread the summer. I need the structure that the school day provides me. Without it, I become overwhelmed. I need down time and time to take care of household business, not to mention my newfound interests.

***

Hello, Summer

Summer is here. This will be my son's last summer before starting high school. How exciting! (I'm so proud!) Time for me to savor mothering him before it's too late. In four short years he'll graduate from high school and leave for college.

No doubt we'll be hitting the mountain biking trails during the day. He's an avid downhill mountain biker. There is no way I can keep up with him. Even before divalproex, my balance left something to be desired. I've always been something of a klutz. So, I'll leisurely pedal the gentle meandering trails enjoying the view and taking in glorious natural beauty (or cacti and dust) while he races down mountains, rocks, sand, cliffs, and all manner of life and limb threatening terrain.

To enjoy this summer, I must somehow learn how to use social media and keep in contact with my friends without gluing myself to a computing device. It's way too easy to be drawn in al hours of the day and night when I carry my smartphone around as if it is an appendage of my body, of my mind, and of my heart.

There are so, so many gifted bloggers whom I want to read, so many comments to make, so much valuable content to share, so many souls to love. To my dear and valued friends, mental health advocates, writers, poets, artists, and kindred spirits with whom I regularly communicate throughout the day and often into the night, summer has begun, and now I must focus my time and energy on my son and on painting our house. Oh, did I mention that I've avoided finishing painting the interior of our house for coming up on a year now? Hi, my name is Kitt. I live with bipolar disorder, surrounded by unfinished well-intentioned household projects. Typical.

Instead of spending this summer typing at my keyboard, I plan to be bicycling on a dirt trail, struggling to keep up with my son, or covered from head to toe with paint (hopefully some ends up on the walls).

Happy Summer. Not checking out entirely, just cutting back, way back.

W sh me luck.

***

Lazy Summer Days

Okay, so I've not exactly kept to my commitment to get outside and play, nor have I gotten any interior painting done. My son has played video games since he got out of school for the summer last Wednesday, his last summer before high school!

I've taken advantage of his laziness and have fallen in step, or rather maintained my own lazy lifestyle at my computer as he is at his. We are pathetic! At first, he played his computer games in the family room. Now he has moved his base of operations back into his room. He goes through phases. Wonder when, or if, I'll see him again this summer. Just joking.

Our huge accomplishment yesterday was readying the gas barbecue for my husband. We tag-teamed it. Much of the interior elements had simply disintegrated, so I removed the dregs and we replaced them with lava rock from our landscaping. My son selected, cleaned, and artfully arranged the lava rock in the barbecue. The resulting, evenly distributed heat made for delicious steaks grilled by my husband.

Okay, my son just came down for a visit; turns out he is researching for our mountain biking trip this summer. He loves studying videos of other bikers, and of the trails he plans on riding. Actually, he's also been researching all sorts of interesting scientific facts which he rattles off: "Did you know...?" No, I did not know... Fact of the day is...

Son: "Guess what the most surprising dominant gene is?"

Me: "I don't know."

Son: "Guess."

Me: "Blue eyes, brown eyes, height…"

Son: "Six fingers. The dominant gene is for six fingers, not five. But nearly no one has the dominant gene in their gene pool."

So far today I have learned nifty new scientific facts, watched a re-enactment of Star Wars IV using only text characters thanks to my son's prodding, sat at my computer reading and writing, ran errands, went to a couple of doctors' appointments, and dead-headed my roses.

***

Artist with Limits

I am an artist with limits

I cannot do everything

I cannot be there for everyone

I am a mother

I am a wife

I am an artist with limits

237

***

Dragging My Knuckles

Yesterday saw my nephew off at the airport. Now I'm dragging my knuckles on the ground. Headaches. Fatigued. Basically, I'm drained.

Have group later this afternoon. Psychiatrist's psychotherapy group members decided to take July off. Not sure how many will actually show up this afternoon. So now I have group therapy on Tuesday afternoon and NAMI Peer-to-Peer hosted by MHA-OC on Wednesday afternoon. Plenty of mental health resources for the week.

The groups will take me away from my son, though, which he does not like. At 14, he's old enough to be left alone, but he prefers that I'm nearby should he need me (should he need anything). During the school year I would go to a writer's group on Tuesday after group and another on Thursday morning. But summer throws me off my game. My son perceives me as always being gone should I go to the writer's groups.

To top things off, this past weekend we visited my parents. My parents enjoyed seeing their two oldest grandsons, but it exhausted my mother, who recently completed a round of radiation after completing her latest round of chemotherapy with Rituxan, monoclonal antibody therapy, of which she was part of the initial clinical trials many years ago. She has lived with non-Hodgkin's lymphoma at varying stages (remission to stage 4) for thirty years. But now the tumor in her thigh is tenacious and visible. The recent treatment has softened the tumor, but it remains, at least for now, threatening. By the way, my son considers both his grandmothers heroes; my mom for battling lymphoma, my husband's mother for battling MS.

They are fighters. They live with chronic illnesses. Doing so is truly heroic.

***

My Dad and Dementia

My dad has dementia – not Alzheimer's, the most common type of dementia - but dementia, nonetheless. His dementia has slowly progressed over many years and is greatly exacerbated by his heavy drinking. I am a genetic heir to alcoholism, fear it, and drink minimally because of it.

Because I am feeling pain and anxiety over my father's health, yesterday I spent an inordinate amount of time formatting and reformatting a cut and paste of content [to my website] from the Alzheimer›s Association on how to cope over the holidays. Rather than write from my heart and deal with my angst, I spent hours tweaking HTML code until my post visually pleased me. In that small way, I exercised control, for I am not in control of my father's brain health. I cannot make him stop drinking. I cannot stop his brain deteriorating, and it devastates me, for I love him dearly.

Yesterday I was silent, hiding with my heart heavy, wondering what could be done to help my mother and father face this beast.

***

Brain is a Brain

When I was visiting with my father to celebrate Thanksgiving, he asked me why what he suffers – dementia, a memory disorder, a neurological disorder – is any different than what I have – bipolar disorder, a mental illness, a psychiatric disorder? Why these distinctions? Why is stigma attached to one and not another? Why do so many of us feel compassion for those with dementia and fear those with mental illness?

***

Private? No, Not I

On the one hand:

> *"You own everything that happened to you. Tell your stories. If people wanted you to write warmly about them, they should have behaved better." – Anne Lamott*

On the other hand:

> *"**Confidentiality:** we ask that you keep confidentiality for anyone else who may have played a challenging role in your recovery journey. Even if you don't mention a specific name, be careful that the identity could not be easily inferred due to an immediate relationship, such as parent, etc. This includes facilities and/organizations as well as individuals." – DBSA's Guidelines for Life Unlimited Stories*

Then, there's this: I tend to exaggerate. I do not lie, but I am known to have a flair for the dramatic. When my uncle read my piece about my father's dementia, he became very alarmed, not knowing that my father is still quite sharp. My dad's still smarter than your average bear (Yogi Bear reference, for those not in the know). Both of my parents are smart cookies.

240

Today, I use clichéd idioms. By the way, I identify with them both, and not just because they are intelligent (yes, I boast).

My mother and I share personality characteristics. As a mother, as a mother struggling with a chronic illness, I feel compassion. When I was a teen and a young adult, I was brutal in my disdain for her. Motherhood is a thankless vocation.

***

Structure

When my husband or son stay home because they are ill, I lose the structure around which I organize my day and myself. I need the bookends of bringing my son to and from school, having my husband go to work and come home. When they are home needing me, needing attention, needing soup and crackers, I lose something of myself. I feel depleted, exhausted. My boundaries need reinforcement. My sense of self does not thrive under these circumstances. I am not well-suited to be a full-time, around-the-clock caretaker. They've been sick on and off since Christmas. I am so weary.

***

He's Home Sick Again

Had to go pick up my son from school… He made it through two hours… Now back home sick to his stomach, needing to be near a bathroom… Even took him to an acupuncturist last week hoping for an answer, a fix. Beginning of June have appointment with pediatric gastroenterologist. Poor kid.

Nurturing Bath

As I desperately reached out in compassion for others these past ten days, I've neglected myself. I fueled my efforts with hypomanic energy, all the while sick with gastroenteritis and caring for an even sicker son. Poor baby gets gastro badly. So here I address compassion burnout, nurturing others while neglecting oneself. My step today to nurture my self is quite simple. I'm taking a bath.

***

Distraught

Grief that I denied myself now hits me. Now I realize how much compassion I withheld from my husband as I defended myself from pain and from being needed. My prayers go out to my in-laws. The tears flow easily now.

Unfortunately, in my hypomanic flurry of activity of late, I lost control of my anger, my rage. Yesterday morning, I lost my temper with my son when he would not wake up and go to school. I hit him on the arm to raise him. I hurt him. I abused him. He cried. He rolled up into a ball and cried. I forced him to go to school unprepared and emotionally raw. I went into the school's office. I spoke frankly with his guidance counselor. I emailed the school psychologist at her recommendation.

My son has given me the silent treatment since the incident. I deserve his silence and worse.

Distraught over my behavior, yesterday I twice called NAMI Orange County's Warm Line. Last night, as I left the house to cool off, I made a voice recording, here transcribed.

***

PARENTING FAIL SELF-CARE FAIL TRANSCRIPT

Okay, today has been a complete parenting fail and failure to take care of myself so that I can be a better parent.

My son's been sick a lot recently. Every winter, every spring, he gets sick A LOT. I've taken him to doctors. Still, he gets sick. Every year he starts out in the fall getting straight A's, and then in the spring, he has to do a whole bunch of catch up because of his absences.

Well, now he's in high school, and he's in like hard core International Baccalaureate and AP classes. I mean all honors classes. And, today, last week he was sick.

Yesterday he went to school, but he didn't do all his homework. He said he had it under control. He didn't. He asked to wake up early this morning to complete an English project. Wasn't able to do the project. Curled up in a ball. Didn't want to do it. Said he was tired.

My husband said he was up all night awake. I don't know what the deal is there. But, he kept on falling asleep, curling up in a ball, wouldn't get up, wouldn't wake up, wouldn't do the homework, wouldn't get ready for school.

So, I just smacked him with my hand. Wrong. Abusive. I gave him a smack sideways. Hit his arm. He started to cry. Okay, you're awake. Do your homework. Get ready for school. We've got to go. You can't miss school. Not doing your homework is not an excused absence. I can't take you to the doctor for an excuse for not doing your homework. Because at this point, I have to take him to the doctor every FUCKING time he is absent from school because he is beyond the allotted absences.

Okay. He cries. He crawls up more, tighter, he is in a little fetal ball. I swat his bottom. I hit him again. I say, you've got to go to school. I don't care you're not done with this project. I'm going to print it out as is. I don't care if it's not done. You can't not go to school. You can't miss your first period in order to do the homework for your second period. You have to go to school.

So, I took him to school. He's distraught. He ignores me. He...

I walk, because I want to go to see the guidance counselor or somebody about the whole situation because I'm just out of my wits. I go.

He ignores me all the way to class walking from the car. He walks a different way.

I go to the guidance counselor. I tell her the situation, the history. We take a look at what his teachers recommended for next year.

Two teachers recommended honors classes – in the classes that aren't even his best classes, like English, his class that he just... is really hard for him to do, is like pulling teeth. He writes beautifully, but getting up in front of people and reading what he writes and writing very intense, metaphorical stuff, not so easy for him. So, he's in this, like, advanced class, where he probably doesn't belong. So, he's... They recommend that. They recommend another AP history. They recommend the honors English. Math, though, his best subject, now recommended regular Algebra 2. Because he's getting a C, because he's been absent.

Fuck. I don't actually care. He can be in all regular classes. But it makes no sense for him to be in honors classes on the classes that are most difficult for him, or at least not in the classes that he has the most passion for but has missed the most.

Oh he's missed them all. But, you know, I mean, you can read something, you can do your history. But, you really, if the teacher teaches something differently than the book is. And, Honors Geometry, he keeps on saying the teacher teaches it differently than the technique in the book. And, when my husband tries to teach it, my husband's an engineer, the way that he teaches it to people... Whatever.

So, major fail. I'm completely distraught. I blew up this evening at my husband over this whole situation.

Guidance counselor says maybe independent study, maybe a smaller private school, maybe, you know, whatever different options. Get him assessed by the psychologist. Get him special ed.

Kid has been in treatment since he was four years old. I'm fed up. I'm fed up. Fed up with taking him to doctors.

I will keep on taking him to his psychiatrist and to a psychologist. I will do what I can to try and get him well, but I am so fed up. I am so fed up with trying to drag this kid to school. I am so fed up with trying to drag him to do homework. I am so fed up with setting limits around video playing when he gets so obsessed.

I'm just done.

***

Fear of Loss

Thursday night I saw my psychologist over the disaster that was Tuesday. First, I had her listen to the distraught voice recording I made that night. I told her about my son's recurring gastroenteritis. He's suffered from migraines with vomiting since he was a toddler, has gastroesophageal reflux disease (GERD), and gets gastroenteritis regularly during the winter and spring months.

I talked about how the illness and death of a local young woman brought forth defended feelings of grief over the loss of my brother-in-law to lung cancer. My psychologist asked me if I'm afraid of losing my son. I responded I don't think so. Then I described how the woman's small intestines had to be removed, and she died waiting for a small intestine transplant from UCLA. At that point, I broke down sobbing, "Oh, my God!" Yes, that was exactly what I was afraid of. My son is still sick. After all these years. After seeing so many doctors. Still sick. Still vomiting far too much for any boy. Still in pain with debilitating migraines in spite of medication. The young woman's death realized my worst fear – that I might lose my son.

Or May 5th, I'm taking my son to a pediatric neurologist (again), and to a pediatric gastroenterologist on June 1st. Both specialists are affiliated with Children's Hospital. Hopefully they'll have some answers. Please, this time, pray for my son. Him I love most of all.

***

My Kid Gets Migraines

My son has suffered migraines since he was at least two years old. I would regularly get phone calls from daycare to pick him up because he was sick again. We did not know what was happening. We thought that he was getting gastroenteritis, aka "the stomach flu." Then my sister observed that when we celebrated holidays with extended family or friends – every Christmas, every Thanksgiving, every Easter, every birthday party – he would get sick, that he was over-stimulated and overwhelmed.

He still struggles. He still gets debilitating migraine headaches that land him in bed. Now, though, as a teenager, he can tell us whether his illness is gastroenteritis or migraines. He can tell the difference. He knows what he needs to recuperate from a migraine – usually sleep in a dark, air-conditioned room, with a cool, damp cloth over his eyes, sometimes ibuprofen or acetaminophen.

Migraines are still much of a mystery. We have much to learn.

***

Migraines - What a Pain!

So, it is May, Mental Health Awareness Month, and I'm not motivated to write about mental health. Not mine, at least. Instead, I find myself drawn to write about parenting a son who has suffered severe migraines since he was a toddler.

My son's earliest migraines involved gastrointestinal symptoms, but no headaches. When he was a toddler, he would throw up for three days straight during and following holidays and play dates. At first, we thought he got sick with gastroenteritis every holiday, but my sister pointed out the pattern and that he was reacting to being overwhelmed.

> *Migraine is not just a bad headache. It is a neurological disease, with head pain and associated symptoms, such as nausea, vomiting, dizziness, sensitivity to touch, sound, light, and odors, abdominal pain, and mood changes. While children generally have fewer and shorter migraine attacks than adult sufferers, childhood migraine can be just as disabling, and it can seriously affect the child's quality of life. -Migraine Research Foundation*

So, this post has nothing to do with bipolar disorder. I write about myself, but it is my son to whom I devote most of my time and energy. I hope and pray that our recent visit to his pediatric neurologist, who recommended increasing his preventive medication, will result in fewer and less severe headaches. It breaks my heart to see my son suffer.

Now that my son is old enough to take a more active role in managing his migraines, now that he can articulate what works, what doesn't work, and what he needs, I finally can admit that mothering him has been hard. I've felt like a failure as I've sought help for him.

Please do not give me advice on what has worked for you or someone you know. We are getting very high-quality help. But, migraines do not magically disappear when you stop eating gluten or go to a chiropractor. Believe me. We've tried (and he's going to an acupuncturist this time round).

Medication works. Hydration and eating protein helps. Not overdoing it helps. Avoiding loud noises helps. Avoiding overstimulation helps. Learning how to cope with stressors, how to know and heed his own limits, well, I hope he develops those skills in therapy. That is his job. He is an adolescent. Some things he must learn to do on his own now.

***

Taking a Step Forward

Today I took a step forward. I went to my psychiatrist. He adjusted my medications, putting me back on a low dose of escitalopram. Monday, we see a psychologist with our son to get some coaching on negotiating our battles and setting some reasonable boundaries.

Called NAMI Orange County's Warm Line and briefly talked to a mentor. Looked into going to Orange County's Wellness Center, which offers all kinds of support and activities, but I'm just not up to making the twenty-mile drive to the City of Orange. Maybe tomorrow I will drive up to The Wellness Center; then again, maybe not. I actually think that I may be sick, physically ill, which is exacerbating my depressive symptoms.

Yesterday I both called and emailed Saddleback Church, which offers support groups and is very close to my home. The main problem I have with Saddleback is that I'm very liberal, theologically liberal, socially liberal, and politically liberal. Saddleback is not.

Just got a call from the nurse's office at my son's school. Had to go and get him. He has a headache and feels sick, nauseated. Honestly, I feel pretty run down myself. And, so it goes…

Taking it one step at a time.

***

Prayer for Healing

My son has been sick way too much this year. He is sick again, this time only with a cold virus, but resulting in another school absence. This year seems to be a record year for pollen and viruses. Add to that the stress of beginning high school with a challenging course load and a death in the family, depression, and a weakened immune system seems to be the result.

My son also suffers from chronic migraines, another burden no child, teen, or adult should have. I'm having trouble relaxing, for I'm worried, which doesn't help much. Anyway, Monday we're visiting a highly recommended pediatric gastroenterologist from Children's Hospital to address whatever harm his lifetime of gastrointestinal migraines and recurrent bouts of stomach flu have had on his GI tract.

***

Chronic Illness is Chronic Illness is Chronic Illness

Chronic illness is chronic illness is chronic illness. I so wish that I had a magic wand that could make my son better, that would stop his migraines, asthma, eczema, allergies, depression, anxiety, gastroesophageal reflux disease (GERD), and stop him from getting every single virus that comes to town. But, I simply do not. I've taken him to numerous specialists ever since he was very young, and he still gets sick A LOT.

I get tired of people expecting me to find some magic potion, simple answer or a cure. There is NONE. We treat, we manage, we medicate, but he remains sensitive. Tried acupuncture. He was not a fan. Tried psychotherapy over the years. He doesn't find it helpful. I am exhausted. Truly exhausted.

***

Too Tired to Write

PARENTING IS A BALANCING ACT

Living with mental illness while parenting a child with chronic health issues is a balancing act. When my son was very young, I tried working as well, and ended up hospitalized. I could only juggle so many roles. Recently I've been exhausted. Too involved in attending to my son's health and educational needs to have any energy left over to write blog posts. Instead of writing I've been sharing other people's content on social media and playing with tools to create inspirational quote memes.

As for my son's health, the lab results for his immunological workup were negative, which is good news. We will see his immunologist/allergist tomorrow afternoon. Friday he is scheduled for an esophagogastroduodenoscopy (EGD). How's that for a mouthful. Try saying it three times fast. I can't even say it once. Hopefully the procedure will rule out gastrointestinal processes, such as hiatal hernia or esophagitis. He's already being treated for GERD (gastroesophageal reflux disease).

Since he was sick finals week, he is taking incompletes this semester and taking missed quizzes, tests, and finals this summer. My son's high school agreed to Section 504 accommodations for his illnesses, including gastrointestinal issues and migraines, which led to far too many school absences this past semester. Section 504 of the Rehabilitation Act of 1973 protects individuals with disabilities from discrimination in any program receiving federal funds.

To prepare for my meetings with my son's school, I read the Special Education Rights and Responsibilities (SERR) Manual by Disability Rights California, which summarizes California and federal law, and met with TASK - Team of Advocates for Special Kids. Thank you, TASK and Disability Rights California!

***

Still Exhausted, But Relaxing

Still exhausted, but on vacation in Waldport on the Central Oregon Coast. When we arrived in Portland, before we drove out to the coast, we stopped at the Willamette National Cemetery where my brother-in-law is buried. The cemetery is beautiful, surrounded by trees with a view of the Cascade mountains in the distance. We said goodbye to Don, held hands, and silently prayed. Don, we love you, we miss you. Thank you for your service to our country.

We are visiting my husband's parents and have rented a small charming cottage near their home. If I climb up on top of this cottage's carport, I can see the waves in the distance through the power lines. The skies are overcast and air cool, clean, and damp - a far cry from the sunny, hot, dusty part of California we call home - a wonderful respite, perfect for slowing down and taking a deep breath.

My son and I are recuperating from last week. On Friday, he underwent an endoscopy of his upper gastrointestinal tract (EGD). Both the procedure and the taking of biopsies have left my son with a sore esophagus, making it painful for him to swallow. Poor guy. Hopefully, his esophagus will heal soon, and his post-op pain will be short-lived. His pediatric gastroenterologist said that my son's upper GI tract looked healthy and the photos he took looked good to me (pink and intact, no ulcers), which is reassuring since he has regularly thrown up his whole life, due to migraines, acid reflux, and gastrointestinal illnesses. For the last few years we have medicated him with omeprazole to reduce his acid reflux (GERD).

When we visited my son's pediatric allergist/immunologist, we learned that her assistant misinformed me over the phone that my son's lab work was negative (that his tests showed no immune deficiencies). In fact, his lab results indicated elevated lymphocytes, probably due to a viral sinus infection, which the doctor is treating with nasal irrigation and antihistamine (azelastine) and corticosteroid (fluticasone propionate) nasal sprays.

Worse than the viral sinus infection, my son is deficient in all tests for pneumococcal antibodies, so he received a Prevnar-13 vaccine. Four weeks following his vaccination, he will get follow-up lab work done to see if he has built up antibodies to the 13 Streptococcus pneumoniae the vaccine targets. At that time, his pediatric immunologist also ordered the mono test panel, which includes testing for the Epstein-Barr virus (EBV) and cytomegalovirus (CMV).

The lesson I learned here is not to simply and blindly listen (split infinitive purposefully used) to someone giving you a summary of lab results over the phone. See the results yourself and have them explained to you. My son's lab results clearly showed problems – problems which we are now addressing.

***

Parenting My Teen

So, I decided to change psychotherapists. Not an easy decision for me to make. Except during the nine months we lived in Eugene and the two years we lived in the Mojave Desert, I've seen the same psychologist since my son was four. As my son turns fifteen next week, that's a long-term therapeutic relationship for me. I've seen psychotherapists since I was an eighteen-year-old freshman at UCLA, and in August I turn fifty-two. You do the math. Obviously, I'm well therapized.

Why did I decide to change therapists? Because I need to see someone who loves working with and understands today's adolescents - my adolescent.

This morning I spoke to my previous therapist, thanking her for her help over the years. She asked the name of my new therapist, for in her own words, she was "too old" to work with adolescents and appreciated having an excellent young therapist for adolescent referrals.

Adolescents require a certain youthful optimism and tons of energy. (Please do not attack me for ageism. The truth is, sometimes wisdom is in order, sometimes youthful energy.) When I was in my twenties, I worked with adolescents as a Marriage, Family and Child Counselor. Back then, I had the required vim and vigor. Now, I'm comparatively world-weary. I'm downright exhausted.

***

The Kid's 15

Maybe reentering the workforce will even be good for my son. It is about time that he was more independent of me. The kid is fifteen, after all. He should be able to ride a bike to and from school, even if we live up a ridiculously steep hill where the alternative is to ride in the bike lane along a six - yes, SIX - lane thoroughfare with a 50-mph speed limit. We are even willing to purchase duplicate textbooks for him, though I should have had that included as part of his 504 accommodations.

***

Online High School - An Experiment

My son struggles with multiple health issues: migraines, cyclic vomiting, weak immune system, allergies, eczema, depression, and anxiety. The newly defined spectrum syndrome ALPIM (Anxiety-Laxity-Pain-Immune-Mood) describes his constellation of symptoms, but does not yet give us answers as to how to cure or treat the underlying genetic disorder.

Monday, August 31st, would have been my son's first day back to high school after summer vacation. Unfortunately, he was unable to get out of bed to start the school year. He spent last Sunday night and early Monday morning vomiting. No doubt he is stressed out. He said he was worried about throwing up at school. He was probably stressed out about making up his incompletes from last semester. At the end of the school year he was sick and missed taking his finals and completing missed assignments.

I gave my son the option of enrolling in an online high school program, which he chose to do Monday morning as I tried to wake him for school. So last Monday I enrolled him in a k12.com school, California Prep Academy San Diego. My new job is to be his "learning coach," supervising his progress. We'll see how that goes. It's an ongoing process for the two of us.

***

Why I Homeschool

I Don't Bake.

I am not a cookie and bread-baking homeschooler, nor am I homeschooling for religious reasons.

In fact, although I have twice attended a multi-denominational Christian seminary, I remain a skeptical and questioning believer.

No, I'm just a mom, trying her best to find the right fit for her kid.

Then, again, who knows...maybe when the weather cools down, I'll bake some bread or cookies. I've been known to bake cookies. Bread would be a new one for me.

***

Online School Didn't Work Out

I have not failed. I've just found 10,000 ways that won't work. - Thomas A. Edison

Okay, so here's where we are now. Online k12.com high school proved an unsuccessful experiment. My son prefers a teacher directly instruct him, rather than study independently for a series of online quizzes and tests. He needs feedback. He needs to discuss what he is learning, to ask questions and get answers, to be asked questions, to develop his critical reasoning skills.

So, last Friday we went and visited a private school that offers one-on-one attention and flexible scheduling. Once my son finishes one of the courses he is currently taking online, we plan to enroll him in the private school.

I believe in trying things out. If something doesn't work, try something else.

Failure is always an option. Failure is necessary to learning.

***

My Hands are Still Shaking

Thursday, I met with the Campus Director of my son's new school. My hand shook as I wrote out the check for tuition. Haven't paid for school since my son was in daycare, back when I worked outside the home.

Starting Monday, my son will take one class a day, one-on-one with a teacher, different subject each day of the week, and will be responsible for completing a week of homework by the next week's class. When he spends time on campus to complete his work, there is a tutor available to help. We are reintroducing him to a social school setting incrementally. By January, I hope for him to spend Wednesday afternoons there while I volunteer as a NAMI Provider Educator.

Honestly, my hands have shaken ever since Thursday. I hope and pray that this school works for my son. I've heard from my therapist and from my son's neurologist that his new school works well for many kids. I must set aside my bias, in favor of socialization and public schooling, to find the solution that works best for my son in overcoming social anxiety and getting back on track.

***

Back to School at Last

In April, my struggle to get my son back to class after multiple absences came to a crisis point. He fell farther and farther behind in his challenging honors curriculum. He was overwhelmed. I was at my wits' end.

Since then, we had him assessed for special accommodations, which never went into place because he did not go back to his regular high school in the fall. We then enrolled him in online classes, which didn›t work out because he needs teacher feedback. Finally, this week, he started one-on-one private school. Each day, he attends 50 minutes of one-on-one teaching, for which he does one week of homework, either independently at home, or on campus where a tutor is available.

***

Stroke

My mom had a stroke. I'm at the hospital with her now. Prayers welcome. Thank you.

***

Acute Stroke Rehab Starts Now

Today my mother transferred from the hospital to acute rehab. She will be doing 3-5 hours of occupational therapy, physical therapy and speech therapy each day for the next two weeks.

My sister and I are trying to figure out how to best help my parents once she leaves rehab. Wish us well. Thank you for your love, support and prayers.

***

Unraveling

After a week of crisis intervention, starting with calling 911 upon realizing my mom had suffered a stroke last Saturday, I'm coming undone. Time for a break.

Luckily, my sister and I have reserves (husbands and sons) helping us out with our parents today. I plan to go home and take Sunday as a day of rest. Wish me well. Wish us well. Keep up the prayers. Thank you.

***

Shut Up Mind, Let Me Rest

Woke up in the wee hours of the morning. Mind won't let me rest. Too many loose ends to tie. Found lovely memory care for both my parents in my neighborhood, so they can stay together, and I can visit regularly. Today must get durable power of attorney signed and notarized, so my sister and I can pay the bills. Praying my mom passes her stroke swallow test. She cannot join my father in memory care unless she can swallow liquids. Continued well wishes and prayers welcome. Certainly, can't hurt. Thank you.

***

Dementia Stroke Caretaking Update

Okay, folks, so here's the deal. It is Thursday. My mom had a stroke probably three weeks ago, maybe the Friday (sigh) before Thanksgiving, and or two weeks. I don't know. I lost track. A week before Thanksgiving.

Quick video update as I run errands and juggle caring for my mom, dad and son. Don't forget I'm married and live with bipolar disorder. Thank God I'm holding it together so far.

***

VIDEO TRANSCRIPT

It's a week after Thanksgiving right now. I'm exhausted.

My sister and I have been tag-teaming and teaming to take care of our parents. Just drove my sister to the airport. Said goodbye. She's going back to her family, who need her.

And I just went shopping for some things for my mom to help her with her stroke recovery. You know, crossword puzzles, not that she will be able to do them yet. But to remind her of what she used to do; she's a big crossword puzzle player. Different pens. I wanted to get some connect the dots, and we ordered something on Amazon, we haven't gotten that yet.

But, anyway, I got her some stuff, some activities to keep her busy in rehab. They'll be doing lots of work with her in rehab.

Brought my parents closer to where I live, so I can go back to taking care of my son and living at home.

So, all your support and well wishes and prayers are greatly appreciated.

Thank you.

We're continuing… we're continuing. My mom has a long road ahead of her, and I'm just going to help her the best I can while taking care of myself and my son.

So, I just wanted to give you an update. There you go.

***

Finally, I Cry

Monday, I joined my mother for music therapy, after which I told her I had to take my son to school. I had a few hours before his class began, but I needed a break. Tuesday, I didn't visit either of my parents. I cared only for my son and myself. Today I sit in the car as my son takes his one-hour class, and I allow myself to cry.

***

Insomnia - My Mind Will Not Rest

My hypomanic racing thoughts can lead to finding solutions, but my racing mind will not let me sleep.

4:15 am: third time I awoke this evening. My mind will not rest, will not cease looking for solutions to our family's health crisis, to my mother's stroke, and to my father's dementia. Unfortunately, crises can trigger mood cycling, for me hypomania.

Grief is a bitch.

I worry, too, about my son. My husband took last week and this week off work to pinch hit for me at home.

***

Thank You

Thank you to everyone who has helped with my parents recently: para-medics, nurses, doctors, physical and speech therapists, and caregivers. Grateful for the excellent care my mom has received.

Most of all, I thank my sister and our husbands. My sister and I worked as a team. Couldn't have done it without her. Our husbands backed us up, taking time off work to care for our kids while we were away from home caring for our parents.

Thank you, care team. Thank you, family. Thank you, community.

***

Guilt Rears Its Head

Even with caregiver help, it's been tough. Friday, one of my mother's occu-pational therapists told me she had asked nursing staff if my mother had been receiving any visitors. After being "on" since November 14th, I took time "off" to recuperate. My mother did not respond well. She refused to go to physical therapy, and instead packed her bags. After a nurse called me, I raced over with my father to calm her down. Tough. I'm wracked with guilt.

***

Stop this Circus - Prayer Request

The last few days have been a circus.

My father made a run for it from memory care, setting off the alarm as he left the building to look for his car in their parking lot, so he could find my mom. The director called me to bring him home with me for the night. Not what I paid for.

My mother has had her bags packed and is quite anxious to get out of the stroke rehab skilled nursing facility. The other day she kept pointing to her wedding band.

Today I visited board and care facilities, looking for a setting that could accommodate them both now. Please pray for a solution as soon as possible. They need to be reunited.

***

Time for Geriatric Psychiatric Hospitalization

Tuesday, I took my mother from her stroke rehab to the hospital for a swallow test. When we returned to her stroke rehab afterwards, she refused to get out of my car. She went so far as to throw my car into park when I was driving toward the entrance. I warned her that her behavior was dangerous, and that if she continued she might end up psychiatrically hospitalized.

To get my mom out of my car, the stroke rehab facility had up to ten different staff members try to cajole her out of the car and back to her room. Two Orange County sheriffs were called to see if she would listen to them (not really their job).

Finally, the paramedics came. A handsome young paramedic took my mother's vitals and monitored her heart rate. She refused a wheelchair and pointed to their gurney. After a three-hour standoff, the paramedics wheeled her back into the rehab facility on a gurney.

On Wednesday, my mother's rehab doctor called and informed me that she refused food, drink, medication, and all stroke rehab treatment (speech, occupational and physical therapy). He recommended a psychiatric evaluation and checked for a urinary tract infection (UTI) which can result in confusion, a delirium-like state, agitation, hallucinations and behavioral changes.

After her psychiatric evaluation, she was transferred to a small inpatient psychiatric facility with expertise in working with geriatric patients. Maybe my mother will finally get the help that she needs. Unfortunately, psychiatric hospitalization relies heavily on group therapy, a format which she cannot benefit from, for she cannot talk due to her stroke.

***

I, Too, Have Lost My Voice

In a seemingly ironic twist of fate, not only is my mother without words without speech due to her stroke, but now I have fallen prey to an upper respiratory infection (cold or what have you) and cannot speak, at least doing so hurts my throat.

So, I lay in bed bored, wishing I felt well enough to do Christmas shopping, which I have put off. I'm a terrible holiday shopper. I started to shop online. While that works for much stuff, I know that I can find cheaper clothes for my son and other family members in local discount stores. So, I hope that I feel better in the next day or two to do my shopping before Christmas sneaks up on us.

Meanwhile, I feel guilty that my mother is psychiatrically hospitalized. I have not visited, for two reasons. The last time I visited her at stroke rehab, she became quite agitated and refused to get out of my car. Even if seeing me didn't upset her, I am sick, and her immune system has been compromised not just by age, but by three decades of fighting lymphoma. An upper respiratory infection could literally kill her.

I should nap, but find it difficult to do so. Worry that I won't be able to fall asleep at night if I nap. But I am sick (and tired), so I should rest.

***

Thumper's Healing, Too

Sick in bed, eating blueberries, drinking tea with honey, sage and thyme, downing cinnamon, turmeric, and oregano oil supplements, and spritzing throat with homeopathic zinc spray. Hubby just brought me Cup Noodles (could have sworn there was an 'o in the brand name, perhaps Nissin brand doesn't use the 'o). Yes, I know that the ramen noodles are not particularly healthy, but it's quick and hits the spot when you have a cold. Once I finish the blueberries, I have a couple of tangerines waiting. My neighbors' tree fruits abundantly.

Dogs are barking. Thumper had a growth removed on Thursday. He mustn't jump up and down, for it pulls at his stitches. Hope that the laboratory results for the growth come back negative (benign). He and Coco were working on removing the tumor themselves, something they do not do with fatty growths or sebaceous cysts. The growth was bleeding and angry looking. Thumper would scratch it and Coco would lick it.

Now Thumper is wearing my NAMIWalks tee shirt, to keep Coco from licking his sutures. Since Thumper has done some running about, the shirt now has blood stains. Need to keep my big boy (he's a huge labradoodle) from running, jumping, and playing with his smaller, younger playmate Coco. Together they get worked up protecting our home from all possible trespassers, human and animal. They spend the day barking at the neighbor's dogs, pacing back and forth, and jumping up and down at the fence line dividing our yards. Coco jumps so high that he gets 3/4 of his body above the 5' fence to see his two canine antagonists on the other side.

***

My Parents Are Still Apart

Overwhelmed with feelings of guilt. Trying to do the best I can. The assisted living memory care, where my father has been staying, cannot accommodate my mother's difficulty swallowing liquids due to her stroke.

My mother is back in skilled nursing after a psychiatric stay for major depression and behavioral changes, due to a UTI (urinary tract infection which can result in confusion or delirium-like state, agitation, hallucinations, other behavioral changes, poor motor skills or dizziness, and falling).

For now, my father remains in memory care. When I first looked at senior care options, I did not even consider looking at board and care homes for my parents, for I imagined them to be crowded and depressing. I only had in mind what the worst homes are like. There are nice homes. Of course, they cost more.

A beautiful brand-new board and care home close to my home can take them both, but it does not yet have its license. Once there, my parents will live in a two-room suite with a private Jack and Jill bathroom and sliders from both rooms to the backyard. My mother loves flowers, so I plan to plant some with her. Now the yard is simply walkway and lawn.

Kills me that it is taking so long to get the two of them back together.

My dad keeps saying he wants to move back to the beach, but I cannot oversee their care from our home and my son is adamant about not wanting to move again. We've moved our son far too many times. He attended five elementary schools. That's four too many. We promised him we would not move again once we returned to Mission Viejo from the Mojave Desert.

My parents' home is not senior friendly. Three stories tall, it presents fall risks. Significant deferred maintenance needs to be addressed. As kitchen appliances have failed over the years, my mother bought toaster ovens to cook. My greatest fear is that if my parents returned to their home, they would go back to drinking, which means that my father would again fall down the stairs (he does so at least once each time we visit).

***

Change is Anxiety Provoking

Great news. Monday I am moving my parents into shared rooms - and most importantly, a shared bed - at a board and care close to my home. To that end, I've been busy with electronic paperwork, and facilitating the transfer of my mother from skilled nursing stroke rehab, and my father from assisted living memory care. Delegated the moving of queen size bed and my parents' clothing to my husband. Sunday, we move the bed and clothes, and I sign the papers and cut the check.

This change, which I expect to be wonderful (which I hope to be wonderful for both my parents and my own family) is still anxiety provoking. So much is riding on it. I pray my parents are happy with the set-up.

Anyway, I've been so stressed out that I've colored a crap load of images, using an app on my tablet, in the last few days.

Today I finally took a clonazepam, hoping it would help. Nada. No difference. I feel like I'm about ready to jump out of my skin. Instead, I write and share with you how moving someone else affects me.

You can imagine how hard it might be to move myself, son, and husband. Whenever I have moved in the last ten years, and we've moved numerous times, I've had a set-back, experiencing deep, and sometimes debilitating depression.

We moved our son five times during elementary school. He, too, is sensitive to change. My childhood growing up, we constantly moved. Because of it, I tend to hold people at arm's length, never getting too attached, for I may be leaving soon.

***

Together Again

Finally, my parents are back together again since my mother had an acute front left lobe stroke in mid-November. We've taken my father to visit my mother in stroke rehab, but tonight they sleep together. No longer is my father in memory care in one facility and my mother in stroke rehab in another.

***

Freaking Out

Once again, I accidentally skipped a medication dose. Thursday evening, I forgot to take my divalproex (used to treat seizures, migraines and bipolar disorder), making me less stable, more irritable, short-tempered with my husband, overwhelmed, emotionally fragile, raw, and vulnerable. F*ck. So that's a bit of background for how I felt Friday and Saturday.

Am I doing right by my parents? Am I failing myself and my son?

***

Friday Texts to Owner of Board and Care

Kitt: My mother's speech therapist told me to work with my mom daily. I'm not up to that b/c I have bipolar disorder and my son gets sick, migraines, depression & anxiety. I must protect myself and my family's well-being. I do not think that the caregivers are up to speech therapy exercises. Maybe I underestimate them.

Owner: Hi, Kitt, I completely understand your concerns & your concerns for your family. I agree with your assessment that caregivers are not really well qualified to do that, but they can try doing it, & we will see how it goes. It will get better.

***

FRIDAY TEXTS WITH MY SISTER

Me: FYI, the speech therapist today said I should work with mom every day on speech therapy exercises. Staff at board and care are just "caregivers." They cook, clean, help with bathing. I talked dad into showering today with mom's help. Mom refused to shower.

Sister: I wonder why mom won't take a shower? You do not need to follow the demands of a speech therapist. You can do the speech therapy exercises when you are available. They will not control your life. You will control your life and time.

Me: This is what she wrote [shared photo of our mother's note with my sister]. Do not know what she meant.

She is having trouble with receptive speech, with understanding what is said to her or asked of her. But she knew we wanted her to shower b/c she gets gestures and if restate putting in context.

Sister: Do you think she needs a chair in the shower?

Me: I bought one. It's in their shower.

Sister: Maybe she wants it out then? Or she's worried dad is going to jump her? love in the shower?

Me: If she wanted it out, she could take it out.

Sister: Yeah. Probably more the second idea?

Me: Thanks for the smile. I'm pretty stressed. I know you are, too. On the positive side, she made huge strides after one session with this guy.

Sister: Good!

***

Hope that Speech Therapy Books Will Help

Purchased three speech therapy books online. Hope that I can delegate exercises for my dad to do with my mom. He has moderate stage dementia, so not sure how it will go. I know he wants to help, though. It will give them something to do together that will benefit them both cognitively. Obviously, I'll have to break it down simply. Will get them a calendar with instructions (page x in book y), shower schedule, and physical therapy and speech therapy schedules.

***

I Said "No!"

My mother's speech therapist (a great guy and excellent speech therapist) called me today so that I could participate in her speech therapy. Friday, when I first met with him and my parents, he told me to work with my mother daily. Afterwards, I freaked out, was bitchy and short-tempered with my husband and son, and finally called my sister, who reminded me that I do not have to do what the speech therapist tells me to do.

Tuesday when he called, I was too busy to join them. My son had school (or at least was scheduled to attend school, he got a migraine and stayed in bed). My father's brother and sister were visiting from Chicago. And, I had psychotherapy (which I needed). So, I told him that I could not make it.

He called again this morning. At first, I agreed to meet him at my parents' board and care. Then, I thought, no, I need to relax today. Tuesday was eventful. Wednesday, even more so.

Yesterday I arranged for my son to Skype his morning class (I forget why he struggled yesterday. Each day is a new struggle.). Then I sat on the panel as a (former) mental health provider (I am a licensed Marriage and Family Therapist who maintains her license but hasn't practiced psycho-therapy for over two decades) to teach NAMI's Provider Education course (teaching it every Wednesday afternoon this month through the first week of February). Then, I had dinner with my husband, aunt and uncle. VERY BUSY day for me. Social demands stress me. I needed to recuperate.

Needing moral support, I talked to my son who agreed I should cancel (not his job to offer me moral support, but he was handy). He, after all, is sick again today, and he is my primary responsibility (yes, I know, I'm not his responsibility, but I need him to help more now). So, I called the speech therapist back and told him I couldn't participate in my mother's speech therapy due to my need to take care of myself (as I have bipolar disorder) and my son (as he has chronic health issues). He was very understanding. Afterwards, I called my sister for congratulations which she enthusiastically gave me. Yay!

***

Day from Hell

Thank you, Friends, for your support!

Recently my mother slammed the door on her speech therapist. She refused nursing care for herself and blocked nurses from seeing my father. Her behavior has caused both of them to be discharged as patients from home health services. No more home nursing visits, physical therapy, or speech therapy.

My parents reside in a board and care near my home, where they are fed and cared for by caregivers. They still are seen by an internist with expertise in treating seniors. They take their medications. And, I have requested that a psychiatrist see my mother.

Back to the story about my mom. When I visited, my mom restrained me and blocked me from leaving their room. My husband felt compassion for my parents and questioned whether they received adequate care (they do). (He supports me now and tries not to offer opinions or "fixes.") I ended up feeling so out of control and overwhelmed that I posted this to Facebook:

I really need a friend right now. Feeling alone, isolated, misunderstood, on my own, unsupported, inadequate.

I received just what I needed - love and support. Here are responses I posted:

Today I heard that my mom's home health care providers were discharging her as a patient because she refuses service and slammed the door in their faces. I'm working so hard to help and feel so helpless. Hard to just let it be.

I'm stressed out caring for my parents and for my son. Got to me. Just broke down. Feeling better, but the weight of my responsibilities remains. Must let go.

Thank you, friends! Greatly appreciate all the support. My feeling isolated passed. You all helped. Spoke to my dear neighbor. In the midst of family crisis. Will be ongoing for a while. Stress can weigh too much and wear me down at times. Sometimes I throw up my arms and cry for help. Thanks for answering my cry.

All the love is loud and clear. The mood has passed. The stressors and triggers remain. Must let go of what I cannot control.

***

Grief, Compassion and Love

Grief can be the garden of compassion. If you keep your heart open through everything, your pain can become your greatest ally in your life's search for love and wisdom. -Rumi

Today my husband flew up to visit his brother, who is at home receiving hospice care for advanced lung cancer, which has aggressively metastasized. This post serves as a prayer for my husband, his brother, and the rest of their family. I'm at a loss for words.

***

I've Got This... Really, I Do

Since my mother refused post-stroke treatment, behavior I could not control, I've been really busy. Bordering on mildly hypomanic at times, yet surprisingly stable, given all the stress I'm under, I gained a sense of control by learning what I can about those things I can control.

Using skills I acquired in my careers in psychotherapy, commercial real estate, and the law (granted, I was a legal assistant specializing in complex computerized litigation, not estates and trusts), I'm doing due diligence to be a good -- no, an excellent -- health care agent and advocate, power of attorney and trustee for my parents. These roles I share with my sister, who is relocating out of state (lucky woman, actually, she's stressed out, too).

The past three weekends, I've met with several real estate agents, brokers, and property managers. Now we're looking at rehabbing and renting out my parents' beach home.

Friday, after speaking to a gerontological psychologist, who will meet with my parents next week, I visited a dedicated memory care community. Hate to keep moving my parents from facility to facility, but must find the right fit for them. My mom needs proper care.

My mother is receiving excellent care in their board and care, but it offers caregiving only, not specialized support or structured activities. My mother is not in control of her life right now and is losing hope for recovery. Before her stroke, my mother had panic attacks, social anxiety, and some distorted thoughts. The stroke injured her brain's front left lobe, exacerbating psychiatric symptoms and interfering with impulse control.

These traumatic brain injuries are trying for anyone. My mother and father were both first-born, high-achievers (as was I). Before her stroke, my mother always had to be in control, and like me, sometimes blew up when overstimulated by social contact or when criticized. Not being able to express herself verbally, (she was former university debate team captain) or get her way, must be a nightmare for her.

***

I've Been Really Busy

Took the time to walk on the beach.

I haven't been blogging as much recently because I've simply been too busy to do so. Moved my parents into a memory care community Wednesday. My parents are getting excellent care there. Already they have participated in the social hour and taken a Zumba exercise class. The caregivers are attentive. They have 24-hour nursing staff, and a medical director. Their specialty is working with people with dementia, especially those kicked out of other facilities. They know how to engage their clients positively. They have dogs, cats, birds, and guinea pigs. Two golden retrievers met my parents when we first went in the door. Perfect. My mom sat and pet the guinea pigs, which is very helpful for calming anxiety. I'm hopeful.

Right now, I'm in their house in Hermosa Beach, taking care of business. Many decisions. Much work. Very busy. Working with my sister to make decisions about their home and their belongings with love and discernment. Paying their bills. Doing their income taxes. Managing their finances. I've interviewed real estate agents and brokers, am getting construction bids on deferred maintenance, and finding out what it will take to get the house ready to rent. Yes, I'm super busy. I've earned myself a drink (maybe a beer or hard cider) and a luscious dessert.

***

May He Rest in Peace

Death is not extinguishing the light; it is only putting out the lamp because the dawn has come. —Rabindranath Tagore

My brother-in-law passed yesterday. May he rest in peace.

***

Worries

Here I am at my parents' house interviewing property managers and con-tractors. My stress is not due just to what I have on my plate with my par-ents, their property, and their finances, but to the reactions of those close to me to the risks involved. My husband worries about lawsuits and cost overages. My sister asks shrewd questions. To the extent they are stressed and worried, I must not only address the valid arguments they make; I must handle them. When I must cope, I do cope. When I must listen, I do listen.

***

Rumi on Grief

I saw grief drinking a cup of sorrow and called out, It tastes sweet, does it not? You have caught me, grief answered, and you have ruined my busi-ness. How can I sell sorrow, when you know it's a blessing? —Rumi

There is something both beautiful and sorrowful when someone or some-thing dies. Something spiritual lives on. Love persists and is a blessing. I do not deny the pain of grief, but believe that death is a part of life, and that grief is a part of loving. There is no way to love without experiencing grief at one time or another.

***

Do NOT Smoke!

First, I hope and pray that I can emotionally support my husband as he experiences grief, having lost his oldest brother last week to lung cancer. Grief, anxiety, and the fear of loss is what prompted me to begin writing this blog back in September 2013.

My husband benefitted from visiting his brother before he died. He was able to spend time with him and to come to terms with his imminent death.

DO NOT SMOKE. Please take care of your lungs.

***

Thankful for Support

Thank you to my son, for exercising more independence as I've been busy attending to my parents' affairs; to my husband, for everything from chipping in around the house to loving me deeply and devotedly; to my sister, as we support each other in making decisions on our parents' behalf now that they are unable to do so; to our extended family, for supporting our decisions and loving us; to my friends, neighbors, and online support network, for being there; to my parents' memory care community, for offering my parents' excellent care and me support and respite; and to my mental health providers, for helping me cope.

Much of the support I have access to is thanks to my parents' savings. Few have such resources and do not have access to the same care options. That is tragic. Everyone needs access to excellent health care and excellent long-term care. Not just those fortunate enough to have significant savings (or adequate long-term care insurance) in their senior years.

Honestly, I never could do it without all of you. Thank you. God bless you all.

Clearing Out

Sunday evening, I relaxed after spending the afternoon letting my husband grab his favorite tools from my father's garage before the estate sales company takes everything not now in storage. After consulting with my sister, decided to move and store very little - the rest we will sell or donate to charity. No sense spending a bunch of money on packing, moving, and storage.

Decorated my parents' room at their memory care with my mom's favorite paintings and charcoals. Today, I learned that my father took them down, confused, thinking that they were in a hotel and had to pack up to leave. He asked that I put everything down in writing for him, because he keeps forgetting.

My husband has had fun wearing one of my dad's big straw hats. He insists that he met me years ago in the mid-80s as I studied on the beach. That he was intimidated by my father wearing a big straw hat and sunglasses as he stood on their second-floor deck keeping a watchful eye on his daughter, and her would-be suitor. My dad scared him off back then, but welcomed him in our life when I was thirty-one.

***

Vascular Dementia and Psychosis

My husband, son and I are visiting my sister, her family, and the in-laws (my sister and I married brothers) in Oregon. Beautiful outside. We can see Mt. St. Helens in the distance.

Trying to focus on nature's beauty to give my mind and my soul a break from the burden of taking care of my parents' affairs.

Had to have my mother psychiatrically hospitalized again. Vascular dementia due to her recent stroke, in addition to pre-existing mental illness (she's my mother, I'm her genetic legacy) led to psychosis. Hope that her new medication regimen will improve the quality of her life.

Painful process to watch, seeing someone you love devastated by a stroke. My mother's vascular dementia is worse than my father's dementia. He has no short-term memory and is aware of his memory loss, but still has verbal skills. My mother has lost her ability to communicate, which makes it very difficult for her.

Take care of your brain. Injuries to it can alter your life in terrible ways.

***

I Am Not Ashamed

I am not ashamed that I live with bipolar disorder, a mental illness, a brain disorder. I am not ashamed that I take psychotropic medication. I am not ashamed that my parents are struggling as they age, as their brains and bodies fail them. There is no shame in that. There is no need to hide. No need to keep it a secret.

As I love and respect myself, I love and respect my parents. I assume that my love comes through my writing. I know that others identify with their struggles and with my struggles. I know that it helps to have others for support, to know that you are not alone. There are support groups. Reach out. Get help. Do not try to do it all alone. It's too much to do alone.

***

Two Losses in Three Parts

As I thought about today's writing prompt, to write about a loss, I kept cir-cling back to two losses: the loss of my maternal grandfather and the loss of my expectations and plans for my future. Now, a third one pops into my mind: my husband's loss of his brother. Somehow, I will be circling around these losses in my following two posts. Not sure exactly what this series wil become.

***

Anxious about Dementia

TRANSCRIPT

So here I am, in my car, which is pretty hot. Probably have to open the windows to let in some air. Just going to make it hard for anything to be heard. Oh, oh, that feels good.

Okay. I'm on my way to the Alzheimer's Association of Orange County, or whatever it's called, Alzheimer's dot org of Orange County. ALZ.org for those who want to check out the national Alzheimer's US group. But I'm going to the local OC chapter's educational series. The first one is Basics, Dementia Basics. I'm driving, so 'm not necessarily getting the title totally correct.

283

I'm actually pretty anxious going to it. Anxious because, well, this is pretty emotionally trying for me having both my parents with dementia right now. My mom's struggling with what's called vascular dementia, which is secondary to her stroke, and can be caused by heart problems, blood pressure, high blood pressure. All those things can damage the brain. Right? High blood pressure goes up, damage to the brain. So, and her stroke was the most damaging to the brain. Just horrible.

And, my dad has been struggling with memory loss for many, many years. This last year it's just taken a real dive. He still has his social skills, but his memory is pretty fried, especially his short-term memory. But he's able to reason. His intelligence is there. It's alcohol-related dementia. Some people are more susceptible than others. Have people drinking the same amount of alcohol. One gets cirrhosis. The other gets alcohol-related dementia. The other gets nothing. So, you never know what you're playing with in terms of your deck, and you better take pretty good care of it.

I try to do my best. Well, I don't do my best. I try to do my better. (Laugh) I don't exercise enough. I know that. I'm taking cholesterol meds, rather than strictly adhere to a low-fat diet. I try, I look at the fat content in everything, but I just have my weaknesses, especially since my mom had her stroke. I've put on at least ten pounds, maybe fifteen. I think it's about ten pounds according to my physician since her stroke, and its pounds where you don't want to have it, on your stomach. That's the area that's not good for your heart.

Heart health is what I really have to take a look at now as somebody who is susceptible to stroke. My grandmother died, my maternal grandmother, my mother's mother, died of stroke, and she'd had several TIAs [Transient Ischemic Attack], which are like mini-strokes, before that. So, anyway, just checking in.

***

Stroke and Swallowing

Sunday night I spent the late night and wee hours of the morning at the emergency room with my mother because she had aspirated food and liquids at dinner. She's doing very well now, but is again experiencing dysphagia, or difficulty swallowing after stroke.

When the nurse at my parents' memory care community told me that my mother was coughing up copious liquid, I worried that she may have pneumonia, or at least was at risk of pneumonia. I rushed over to take her to the ER. As soon as I saw her, I knew that she must have recently aspirated food and liquids, for she looked absolutely gorgeous. She obviously was not sick. I've had pneumonia, and I remember how miserable I felt and must have looked.

***

Heavy Heart

Heavy hearts, like heavy clouds in the sky, are best relieved by the letting of a little water. - Christopher Morley

Now that I filed taxes and got my parents settled into their memory care community, I'm able to take a breath and feel the weight of caregiving or me, on my now heavy heart. Struggling with the weight of caregiving for parents with dementia, and a son with migraines while I live with bipolar disorder, the depressive symptoms of which threaten me now.

Hitting a bit of a depressive trough. Not up for much. Maybe, though, it's not bipolar depression, but simply the weight of caregiving, a weight all caregivers feel. Pain. Sorrow. Mourning. Exhaustion.

Feel sluggish with this huge weight bearing down on me. The weight hangs there. The tears I hold back, but feel them just beneath the surface. I let them out only for a few gentle minutes at a time, holding back the flood for the long haul.

***

Exhausted

My body is simply exhausted from the stress and responsibilities I've taken on since my mother had her stroke. I still haven't allowed myself to feel the grief in my heart at her losses. Her sudden plummet into vascular dementia, and loss of speech and language comprehension due to her stroke are absolutely devastating, more so than my father's dementia, which has progressed over time.

Considering spending the weekend at a spa... I need it. I've earned it.

***

Journal Entries - Late April

So here I am writing, journaling, trying to get this burden off my back, out of my chest. Too heavy. Too painful. Not exceedingly so, but like a long keen. Yes, I am keening, mourning the loss of my parents. They are alive, but I mourn their loss of cognition. My husband has brought up a couple of times that we are 25 years away from where our parents are now. Not so far. We must take care of ourselves. I've been neglectful. Have been eating too much sugar and not exercising enough. My husband has been good about walking the dogs. Our son needs to increase his physical activity, as do I.

I just cocoon. Sit on the couch, licking my wounds, my psychic, emotional wounds.

I have to pee…

***

A week has gone by since I last wrote, since I last journaled. My sister visited Sunday. We had lunch with our parents.

Last night my sister and I decided to sell our parents' house. Huge relief. Have interested parties already.

***

So, this is not exactly a journal. Meant to bring one of mine. Looked in spa gift shop and considered buying a gratitude journal. Decided not to. Not sure exactly why, aside from the fact that it simply was not what I wanted. So, here I am writing with my illegible handwriting on the few pages of notepaper in my room.

Moved outside onto the lanai. Patio. Rearranged furniture. Turned down champagne in lobby. Instead accepted a bottle of water, which sits beside me ready to be opened and consumed. Cracked it open. Had a few swigs. Not able to totally succumb to relaxation. Not yet anyway. After mani-pedi, in opposite order, I ate lunch, checked into my room, which turned out to be a bungalow near the spa. Nice.

Then made dinner reservations. Hope dinner is fun, that Sarah Fader and Allie Burke actually do make it here. After making the reservations, I took a walk along the coast. Got my feet a bit dirty, as I was wearing free spa flip flops.

And, there it is: a sigh, a deep inhalation, breathing in sea air and scent of scrub from mani-pedi. I can hear birds all around me, along with the hum of what I guess is an A/C or perhaps pool heater. Not sure what's in front of me, behind the wall, behind the pool/spa building. The building where perhaps, or probably, I'll be getting my massage.

Sheriff helicopter just flew by really close. Getting the running narration out of my head and onto the paper. Not especially interesting. Rather mundane. But must start somewhere. And, feel I must write. Cannot believe I didn't bring journal. Meant to. Or at least to bring laptop. Typing on iPad, even with Anker keyboard, is frustrating. I type too fast. Crap, my handwriting is illegible!

***

Mother's Day Guilt

So here I am once again typing. Still fatigued. In bed. Nick is gathering laundry. I'm lucky to have a husband who will do laundry. Looking forward to a simple breakfast of Cheerios and banana and a strong cup of coffee. Nick's going to make me breakfast and coffee and bring it up to me to enjoy it in bed. He does it every weekend, and I love him even more for it.

Visited my mom and dad yesterday for their memory care community's Mother's Day lunch. When I arrived, I had been told that my parents had been walking around. I arrived a little late, for I stopped for flowers. I found my parents in their room, and my mother was crying. I reassured her that, of course, I was coming to visit her on Mother's Day. I just ran late, for I picked up some flowers. I joined them for lunch in their room, then we took a walk, and sat outside enjoying the day while we ate dessert. The dessert selection was wonderful. Miniature tiramisu, cheesecake topped with fresh fruit and whipped cream, cannoli, and cupcakes.

Wiped me out visiting. Hurts. Deep down. That keening. That slow, long-term grieving. Grieving the parents I had, the mother I knew. Wishing I could talk with her. Wishing I could call. Wishing she could communicate with me. I do my best to decipher her emotions, her body language. I do my best to understand what she tries to say, to show, to write. Terribly painful. Fuck strokes. I'm pissed off that my mother can no longer speak or write. We must communicate non-verbally, using movement and facial expressions.

Complaining too much. At one point last weekend, I fantasized about my own interests, not so much about mom and dad. That's where I need to focus.

***

Mother's Day

Not sure I have anything to say or to write today. Will be a day of rest, and maybe a walk with Nick and the dogs. Would prefer a wilderness walk than a dog walk. Maybe I'll ask Nick and Matthew to go on a hike with me. Maybe I'll just spend the day in bed relaxing. Who knows? When I've walked with Nick and the dogs recently, it's been only for very short walks. Don't really like walking the dogs. Still associate walking them with them attacking other dogs. Still traumatized by the time they viciously attacked a greyhound.

Anyway, not so sure that thinking about that helps. Need to desensitize myself. Nick's been working with the dogs by walking them regularly. Still don't trust them. Always want to come back as soon as Thumper poops. Even though Nick carries the poop bag, not I.

Happy Mother's Day, Kitt! Don't feel so great. What do I need to do to feel better?

Friday, I visited and had lunch with my parents in their room. My mother was crying when I found them in their room. I went up to my mother and reassured her that, of course, I was visiting her for Mother's Day lunch, that I was delayed in arriving because I stopped to buy flowers. Honestly, I had trouble dragging myself out of bed. I hugged her, showed her the flowers I bought. We put them in a vase. Next time, I'll buy an arrangement already in a vase and remove empty vases from her room.

While we were in their room, my mother opened her calendar, pointed to the day, and asked that I write. I wrote, "Kitt visited for Mother's Day" (or something to that effect, probably with fewer words since her calendar is small). She pointed again. I wrote, "ate lunch." She shook her head and tried writing numbers. I asked, "Do you want my phone number?" Yes, she nodded. So, I wrote my phone number, which she copied. I told her, "Good job copying the numbers."

She let me know that she wasn't pleased. I took her to the nurses' station, conveniently next-door to their room. I asked her if she was happy with the 24/7 nursing. She nodded and smiled at the nurse. The nurse walked us to the front desk and brought out an administrator and assistant health director. My parents had already met them, but I wanted to let my mother know that these were the women they could speak to about concerns. My mother took their business cards, which she seemed to appreciate.

Forward to today, Mother's Day. My mother went up to the front desk and adamantly pointed to my phone number. They called and put her on the phone. She seemed okay at first. I reminded her that I had visited Friday and that today I was celebrating Mother's Day with my son. She started crying. I told her I loved her. I reminded her of the flowers I brought and the flowers my sister had sent. She hung up at some point.

I called back to speak to the social worker to ask for advice. The social worker had redirected my mother, reminding her that I had visited Friday. The social worker thinks that my mother becomes overwhelmed on these "special" days and feels isolated. My father doesn't remember whether I've visited. The social worker said she'd write in my mother's calendar that I spoke to my mother on the phone today, which is what I USED to do on Mother's Day.

I'm a mother now, too. Yet, I feel guilty that I am not visiting my mother. Honestly, I feel guilty that she had a stroke. I mourn, as no doubt does she, the phone calls we used to share. I used to communicate with my mother almost daily, either on the phone or through Words with Friends. Now, we cannot really do that. We've lost our former way of relating. We grieve that loss. We have not yet found our new stasis.

Our new normal must begin with my mother and father becoming comfortable with their living arrangement. Every time that I visit, my father asks when they are leaving. At least he seems to have stopped asking my mother's prognosis. At least he asks less often. When he does ask, I tell him that my mother had her stroke in November, that it is now May, six months later. He's intelligent. His short-term memory is blown, but he understands that six months and little improvement does not promise a great prognosis. Yet, I tell him that there is no way I can predict the future. As time goes by, this will become our new normal.

***

What If I Don't Blog About Bipolar?

TODAY I COCOON IN BED

Recently I've been blogging about caregiving and about exhaustion, more than about living with bipolar disorder. That said, obviously coping with major life events, such as taking on the role of caregiver of two parents struggling with dementia, is a HUGE stressor and potential trigger for mood cycling.

Cocooning in bed right now. Treated myself to two luxurious nights on two separate weekends as payment for all the work I've done. I coordinate my parents' care, pay their bills, cleared out their house of their personal belongings with the help of an estate sales company, took multiple construction bids while we considered remodeling and leasing it, and now I'm our sales agent's main contact. Luckily, my parents made an excellent decision when they bought their beach house in the '70s. The proceeds from its sale will enable my sister and I to take care of our parents.

***

Lunch with Mom & Dad

Driving to have lunch with my parents. I'm apprehensive. It's challenging seeing my parents. They're not happy with the decisions I've [we've] made for them. They want to be back in their home, which is in escrow [has since fallen out of escrow]. But, they're not able to take care of themselves. And, I'm not able to take care of them either.

I know they had wanted us to stay in their house, to have us take care of them. But, I have bipolar disorder. My son gets migraines and has social anxiety and depression. My husband would do anything, is willing to do anything. But I don't think it's good for him either to be put in the position of taking care of everybody. He's got some anxiety himself, claustrophobia and he's an engineer, so he's a little tightly wound.

None of us is kind of chill. Let's just put it that way. None of us is chill.

We're thoroughbreds. We're tightly wound. We're a little over-bred for intelligence. You know, sort of the Jack Russell terriers of the world. Anyway, I guess that's it for now. A little cathartic sharing.

***

I'm a Good Daughter, I Promise

WAY BACK FROM VISITING MY PARENTS

VIDEO TRANSCRIPT

Okay. I pulled into a parking lot to adjust the camera. I like driving with the windows open. So, we're going to get a lot of, we're going to get a lot of noise. I guess I could close the windows, but I love the windows open. I close them when I'm with my son because he doesn't like the windows open, so we have air conditioning. But, when Kitt drives [alone], we have the windows open.

Um. Driving back from visiting my parents. Totally intense. Um. My mom refused to eat their mechanically separated food, which is like an aphasia diet, not aphasia, dysphasia. Anyway, swallowing problem diet to prevent her from aspirating her food, which is swallowing her food and liquids going down not the esophagus, but the trachea and into the lungs. Not a good thing. Leads to aspiration pneumonia. Not good. So, stroke you know, can cause dysphagia, this swallowing problem. So, she refused that, and she wanted the lasagna. So, after lunch, or as she was eating lunch. Well, when I was done. She started coughing up her food. So, I brought her to her room. Told the nurse. So, the nurse listened to her lungs. Said her lungs sounded good.

My mom continued for the next couple of hours to cough up liquid and food out of her lungs. Because [sigh], it's so horrible. Stroke, you know, makes it so the brain isn't telling the throat muscles what to do. This is like the non-scientific explanation of post-stroke swallowing difficulties. I think it's dysphasia. I think that's what it's called. Anyway, food goes down trachea to lungs. Not where it belongs, food and liquid. Rather than esophagus to stomach. She coughed it all up, which is good.

And then she wanted to talk to me, and I thought, you know... She also has aphasia. [Actually, I was told recently that she has apraxia. She may have both. I'm no speech and language pathologist.] She's not able to communicate very clearly. So, um, she's thinking, but not able to get those thoughts across because she's not always able to write the words she means or say... She's not always able to say... very few of the words she means.

And, my parents have been isolating in their room, and not participating in the activities that are designed for, you know, vascular dementia and other dementias at their memory care facility. Memory care is a little bit of a misnomer, because they care for all sorts of brain injuries that lead to dementia. And, dementia isn't always memory loss. Or, maybe it is. I don't know. I'll have to look up that definition.

What Is Dementia?

While symptoms of dementia can vary greatly, at least two of the following core mental functions must be significantly impaired to be considered dementia: Memory, Communication and language, Ability to focus and pay attention, Reasoning and judgment, Visual perception. (https://www.alz. org/what-is-dementia.asp)

But, anyway, brain, you know, they have people with temporal lobal [Frontotemporal Dementia (FTD)], you know, anyway, brain injuries [Traumatic Brain Injury] from being football players, brain injuries from surgery, Alzheimer's, alcohol-related dementia, which my dad has. I'm an heir to alcoholism. I can feel it in me. And, I have to be very careful not to drink regularly.

Um. And, my mom had the stroke. My mom had been the caregiver of my dad. And, she had a problem with blood pressure, a-fib, and, um, well, needing blood thinners. Now, she's on a variety of medications to prevent another stroke. Her stroke was pretty severe, and she now has what's called global aphasia.

So, OK, so we met with the social worker. She has a background [master's] in psychology, but she's getting her MSW. Anyway, met to go over, um, to communicate with the three of us. My dad's like Dory, the forgetful fish voiced by Ellen DeGeneres in *Finding Nemo* and *Finding Dory*. He remembers for like a few minutes and then forgets, so he's always having to be reminded. You can't blame him. You know, you can't control it. He's like Dory.

So, my mom got out the word "family" in terms of where she wanted to be. And we had to explain to her that I couldn't take care of her because of my bipolar disorder, I would end up hospitalized. I hardly have my life together, as it is taking care of...this might be a bit too much wind. I can hardly take care of myself, my kid, and my husband, and my house. I mean, it's a mess. Um, and my mom's, she can be challenging. In fact, she's challenged several different places. A lot of places have had trouble with my mom, because she's a pretty strong-willed woman. Um, should have been a CEO or something. Anyway, she was the CEO of our lives. She was a mom.

Anyway. [sigh] I'm, I'm spent. She wanted to continue to talk to me after we had met with Sheila, the liaison, social worker, but, um, I just said I had to go. That it had been, that we had done a lot, and that was, that was enough. That was enough. I kissed her. When she said... Oh, she said the word "family." Did I say that already? She said the word "family." Clearly, and I hugged her and kissed her for saying the word, and said, "I can't."

I know she wants to live with family. Yeah, I know. Wouldn't be good for her. Wouldn't be good for us. It's hard making these decisions. I feel so, I don't know. I'm not even going to say. Say, like, I feel like I'm betraying my mom. I feel callous. I feel selfish. I'm working so hard as is. I mean, really. Even with all of these professional resources at my behest. Using my parents' savings, selling their house, which I know they don't want us to do, but we're doing in order to care for them. I know it's breaking their hearts, but it's what's best for us all. I visit them regularly. I'm a good girl. I'm a good daughter, I promise. See, that's like my thing. Being a good girl.

[Sigh] Oh, God. This is so hard.

***

Friday Was Tough

Yesterday was really intense. We had gotten, or I had received, a call from my parents' memory care that my dad was... my parents were very upset because they were separating them into separate rooms.

There's a good reason for separating them. When together they isolate and don't let caregivers take care of them and don't participate in activities and don't socialize, and their health deteriorates. When they're separated, which we've had them separated at different times since my mother has had a stroke, they both participate in activities in their separate facilities. They actually do better. Both of them.

So, the idea was to have them in the same facility, but in separate rooms with same sex roommates. They can still visit each other. They can still see each other, but they have to sleep separately to try to see if we can break their co-dependent relationship. It's a dynamic that's not unusual. Problem is, they take care of each other and don't let other people take care of them. And, they need help. They can't. They're not really up for taking care of each other. They're not up for taking care of themselves, or each other.

I know that they love one another deeply, and we want to respect that. And, they still have the opportunity to have private time. That's respected, as well. But in order for them to get the most out of the program that we're paying for, they have to participate in it. They have to let caregivers come in. They have to do things that exercise their brain, rather than deteriorate.

If we were to just let them isolate, then I would get the cheapest care possible and just... But I've already seen what that results in, which is unfortunately violent behavior and at times, even now, psychotic behavior for which I've had to have my mom hospitalized a couple of times since her stroke.

The stroke has damaged not only just the part of her brain that handles language, but the part of her brain that handles impulse control. So, any psychiatric illness that I may be heir to, and I am, is exacerbated by the brain damage.

So anyway, I just wanted to put that out there. I have writing that I've done, very scattered, and I want to touch on and that I haven't really talked about, which is about... I'll just go into it... My sister's going to hate me for this. Which is about what it's like growing up in an alcoholic family. How challenging that is. What it's like being raised by a parent who has no insight into her own illness or behavior. How it affects those who love her, and who she loves.

There's no doubt my parents loved us. Very well. Very much. But it was very hard for... I'll speak for my own behalf.

I am thankful very much for my sister for being my reality test. When things seemed really crazy, we'd look at each other and go, this doesn't make any sense. And, that, that's huge. That's huge.

But it's a part of mental illness, not realizing that you have it. Not everybody has insight. Not everybody seeks help. Not everybody gets help. It has a devastating effect on those who love, and are loved by someone with unacknowledged, undiagnosed, untreated mental illness or unacknowledged, undiagnosed, untreated alcoholism, dual diagnosis. It's really tough.

Sometimes children raised in such an environment try desperately to please, thinking they can control behavior they can't control. Hoping that they can earn love and avoid the emotional abuse that may come with behavior that is unpredictable, and that you can't understand what you had done to bring it on, because you hadn't done anything to bring it on.

There you go.

Brain Dead

All three of us – my son, my husband, and me – are sick with a virus of some sort. The flu perhaps. Exhaustion I already felt, now worsened by deep fatigue achy muscles, nausea, and headache. My brain just is not working. Pulling up the wrong words. Not able to construct thoughts.

Still, took my mom to communication recovery group yesterday. Wipes me out to do so, honestly. Have to reconsider it. Another family member in the caregiver support group was familiar with resources and support groups closer to us.

I had tried calling to find out more information about that group earlier, and was told that the group was not open and not communication recovery oriented. Apparently, whoever I spoke to wasn't aware of the communication recovery group in question. Difficult looking for resources and getting the door slammed in your face.

Honestly, I don't know if I'm up to taking my mom to these groups. It helps her, but comes at a cost to me. She and my father insist on going back home, which is not an option. She wants to live with family, which would be devastating. My parents were challenging even before dementia and stroke due to alcoholism and mental illness. We love one another but doing so can be, has been, painful.

***

Father's Day with My Dad

I'm on my way to my parents' memory care to celebrate Father's Day with my dad. Yesterday, when my mother learned that I was going to be celebrating Father's Day with my dad and not be taking her to her communication recovery group in Newport Beach, she became very distraught, cried, and tried to leave the facility. So, got a phone call asking if they could hire somebody to take her to the course. It freed me up to meet with my father for Father's Day.

Granted, I'm not able to take my kid to and from school on Fridays when I go and spend Fridays with my parents. So, whenever I go and spend Fridays with my parents during the week, it interferes with my parenting. Luckily, today my husband's home and he's taking my son to school. My son goes to school too far to ride his bike.

So, I'm anxious because I'll be seeing my mother before she leaves, and I don't know how she's going to react. I'm just anxious because whenever I see them, they expect me to get them out of there (their locked memory care community). And, I can just only take so much of it emotionally. It's very trying.

So, it interferes with my ability to do my passion, which is writing, blogging, which I haven't been doing as much. And, yes, I know people, some people, are a little concerned that I'm doing this while driving. But, it's a long drive. It's like a twenty minute, half hour drive. We're in neighboring cities, but Mission Viejo is a long city. And, then, it takes a while to get from their memory care facility to the Newport Beach communications recovery group.

I just don't want to keep taking my mom. I want to start backing out of being a caregiver. I still basically am. But, I want to start putting up more boundaries and protecting myself, which I had to do before all this. I had to protect myself. I have to protect my time.

I have to make sure I have enough energy to take care of myself and my son. First and foremost. I have nobody else, beside my husband. Yes, my son is an adolescent, but he doesn't drive, and it's just not safe for him to ride his bike to and from school because of super busy streets. The speed limit is like 50 mph. He doesn't feel comfortable riding on these streets. He feels comfortable on mountain trails, but not on these streets.

***

Wrote Folie à Deux

Last Monday I wrote about a delusion shared (folie à deux) by my parents. The delusional thoughts originated from my mother, but my father backed her up, and in doing so, failed to protect us from verbalized delusions, better not shared with one›s children. The delusional thinking was, and still is, disturbing.

Understand that delusional thoughts are a symptom of mental illness, of a brain disorder. When a couple reinforces each other's delusional thoughts, they get stuck in a reinforcing feedback loop. In isolating themselves from others, they fail to test their version of reality against outsiders' views.

My mother lived with an unacknowledged, undiagnosed mental illness. As her daughter, I'm in no position to diagnose her. Loyal and devoted, adoring, in fact, my father always backed my mother up. He might agree (in secret) with us, but then he would make us apologize to our mother for something SHE said, explaining to us that our mother didn't feel appreciated and it was up to us to give her the attention she needed.

Not a healthy dynamic, but by the time we were teenagers, we knew it was not healthy. Thank God, my sister and I had each other to tether ourselves to reality.

As an adult, as a mother, in many ways I identify with my mother. I can see myself in her. I can see my illness in her illness. So, I feel compassion for her. But we differ in how we have dealt with our disordered brains. I had insight and sought treatment early.

As it turns out, since my mother had her stroke, I learned that she was being treated for depression. She told me a few years ago that she took an SSRI for anxiety, for panic attacks, but she told me she stopped cold turkey (dangerous). I was unaware that she went back on them for depression.

***

Writing on a Plane

Visiting in-laws. Being around that many people can be overwhelming, overstimulating. Matthew is likely to get a migraine. We will have nowhere to go for respite aside from the car (and the beach itself).

Tomorrow night and Monday night, when we stay in Newport, we may rent a second car so that Nick can go to and from, and Matthew and I can stay at the hotel and order room service or go shopping, as there is no sales tax.

This is boring. Writing this. Who cares?

***

What am I thinking? I'm thinking that I DO NOT want to be a caregiver. DO NOT want to be blogging about being a caregiver. I was looking forward to having free time to develop my blog, my writing, start speaking. NOT taking care of mom and dad.

So, here I must decide to back off. For my own good. They are being taken care of. I know I will get phone calls. Hopefully less so as mom settles into her latest placement. She's been a challenge to accommodate.

She's doing better now that we've separated her and dad.

So, I will leave her be. Let her adjust. Allow her caregivers, her memory care to do their job. I will back off. I will not go above and beyond the call of duty.

***

What do I do to help Matthew? Fuck it. Fuck taking care of Matthew. I brought meds. Just let him deal. I must figure out how to take care of my-self. I've noticed recently how sensitive I am to external stimulation. I'm raw. Jangly. All nerves. I'm spent. Burned out. Need another spa weekend. Need to recuperate.

Deep breath. Relax.

Perhaps... Perhaps I could turn off my phone more often, or let it go into voicemail when I get calls regarding my mom...

Got to make Matthew get a driver's license. Need him to be able to drive. Realize he's young, but it would really help. Too much to drive him to class for just one hour. Ridiculous, in fact. Perhaps his class schedule could change. How would it best accommodate me, my needs?

***

Matthew keeps on bringing up issues with equipment. We buy him the best, then he complains and asks for more and more and more.

Like mom, a sponge. I must say NO.

NO. You figure it out. You call for technical support. I will not continually buy you new devices. NO. If I can use my computer for over a year and just send it in when it needs repairs (which is a pain in the ass, granted, I admit that it is, and that I've had problems with my laptop screen on more than one occasion).

He and I both use our computers more than most. For most of our waking hours.

***

I am fatigued. Deeply fatigued. I could just sleep and sleep and sleep.

***

My eyes

My eyes struggle

Dry

They hurt

Can't wait to land

Then long drive to coast

Three and a half hours

Will take forever

The day of endless travel

Plus, I can smell shit

Oh, the joy of sitting next to the toilet

Feel like throwing up

Crap

Feel like it

Can smell it

Shit

Feel like it

Smell it

Thank God for flight attendants and air freshener

Much better now

Though still exhausted

Still spent

Need rejuvenation

Need Matthew to start taking better care of himself

Maybe I can pay him to…

I've offered to pay him to take driver's ed

He drags his feet

***

Want to sell minivan

Nick taking forever to "fix" it, to ready it for market or for donation to charity

Want to sell my parents' car, too, though I like driving it, actually

Prefer driving it to the Honda Civic

Makes sense to wait until Matthew is driving to buy new car

Only need two cars

Mistyped only need two cares

Two cares

What two cares do I need?

What two cares can I limit myself to?

Must care for myself

Must care for my marriage

Must care for...

Yes, I must care for Matthew, but less so than before

He'll be sixteen in a couple of weeks

Time to be more independent

Time to push him out of the nest

So is he afraid of driving because he gets migraines?

His school is close...

I think he'll feel safer driving himself than having me drive him

I'm not the best driver in the world

Spacey driver

In my head too much

Do not pay enough attention

Getting ready to descend

Yay!

Time to pack up

Almost

They haven't told us to lock our trays yet

Guess I can type a few more lines of words

Whether or not I have anything of substance to say

Looking forward to being out of airplanes and airports

Looking forward to driving out to the Central Oregon Coast

Beautiful drive

Nick will drive

I will sleep

This time I reserved a mid-size car

No more "Speck"

We always get the cheapest car

Cars so tiny that we can barely fit

Not this time

I insist on being comfortable on this trip

When we arrive

When we are in Newport on Monday morning

We'll have to look into renting an Enterprise car for Nick

Turbulent no

Fasten seat belts

Put tray table back

Not sure if it's about time to pack up my iPad

Anker keyboard works well with Apple Pages app

Many apps it does not work so well with

***

Not sure I have any more words to share, any more words in me right now, but since it's not yet time to pack up my iPad, I'll continue.

Must care for myself. Must distance myself from my mom. For my own good. She drains me. I've always had to protect myself from her, yet I remain enmeshed. Must separate. Feel guilty. Like I'm a bad girl, a bad daughter, a bad person. Like I can never give enough. Yet, the more I give, the less I have left. I cannot give when I end up drained, spent.

***

This I'm not so sure I can share, but here it is. The thought, the wish, that my mother dies to spare me. Extreme. Felt it as a much younger woman. Hatred, anger toward my mother. Love her, too. Complicated. When my mother once stormed out one afternoon, when my sister and I were adolescents, saying she was leaving, moving out. We said goodbye (and thought, good riddance). She, our mother, soon called back home and asked us if we wanted to go to a movie. We said sure, and the three of us went to see *Airplane*. Ambivalent, for sure. I haven't shared in detail the complicated relationship I have with my mother. I am heir to her illness. She never admitted to having a mental illness. She never admitted to ever making a mistake or being wrong. I can't believe that I am still dealing with this shit. That I haven't yet worked through it. My psychiatrist keeps asking me how my sister managed to not get so entrapped and enmeshed. I think it is that she let herself see and feel her anger at our mother, at our parents, early on. I did not. I internalized it. Took it upon myself. Martyred myself.

***

Hands Full

Hands full this week caring for my son. He's going through a rough patch. His migraine medication (anti-seizure medication topiramate aka Topamax) interferes with his memory and cognition (why it's nicknamed "Dopamax"), making it challenging for him to read, complete his homework, or take a test. Especially frustrating for him, for he's gifted (yes, I'm biased and boasting. I'm his mom and I'm proud of him). With his neurologist's input, reduced the dosage of his topiramate. He prefers migraines over not being as bright. Hopefully the reduced dosage will still prevent migraines and lessen or eliminate the side effects.

***

Wave the White Flag

Need to write out the pain and exhaust on in my heart

Pain and grieving my parents' dementias

Pain and exhaustion caring for my son

Must back off both

Must take care of myself

Must

Must

Must

Must take care of myself

Ready to throw in the towel

To admit defeat

To wave a white flag

To say I give up

I give up

I cannot control the chaos that is my life

I cannot heal others

They must help themselves

They must accept or seek help from others

Not just me

I need a break

I am exhausted

I cannot take it anymore

I am not strong

I am broken

I am ready to break

The burden is too great

The weight on my back too heavy

Please take it off me

Please stop

Please give me a break

Please

Please

Please

Stop

Stop

Stop

Please stand up on your own

Please stop asking me to fix you

Please accept that you, too, are broken

Please stop looking to me for help

Please

Please

Please

I cannot do this anymore

I cannot

I cannot

I cannot

Its too much for me

Too much

Too much

Too much

I'm breaking

Under the burden

Fuck this shit

***

P.S. When I free-wrote this I vented. Yes, I'm exhausted, but hanging in there. Just fed up. This is theatrical, I know, but, I wrote how I felt at the time.

P.P.S. My husband made me tea with honey and brought it to me. On his days off, he brings me coffee and Cheerios with banana. I love eating breakfast in bed. Not a morning person. Last night he bought me a box of

Entenmann's chocolate frosted donuts, which I've polished off (one of my favorite indulgences). My sixteen-year-old son popped in and told me he loved me and gave me a hug. I'm appreciated.

***

Nothering, Too Good, or Good Enough Mother?

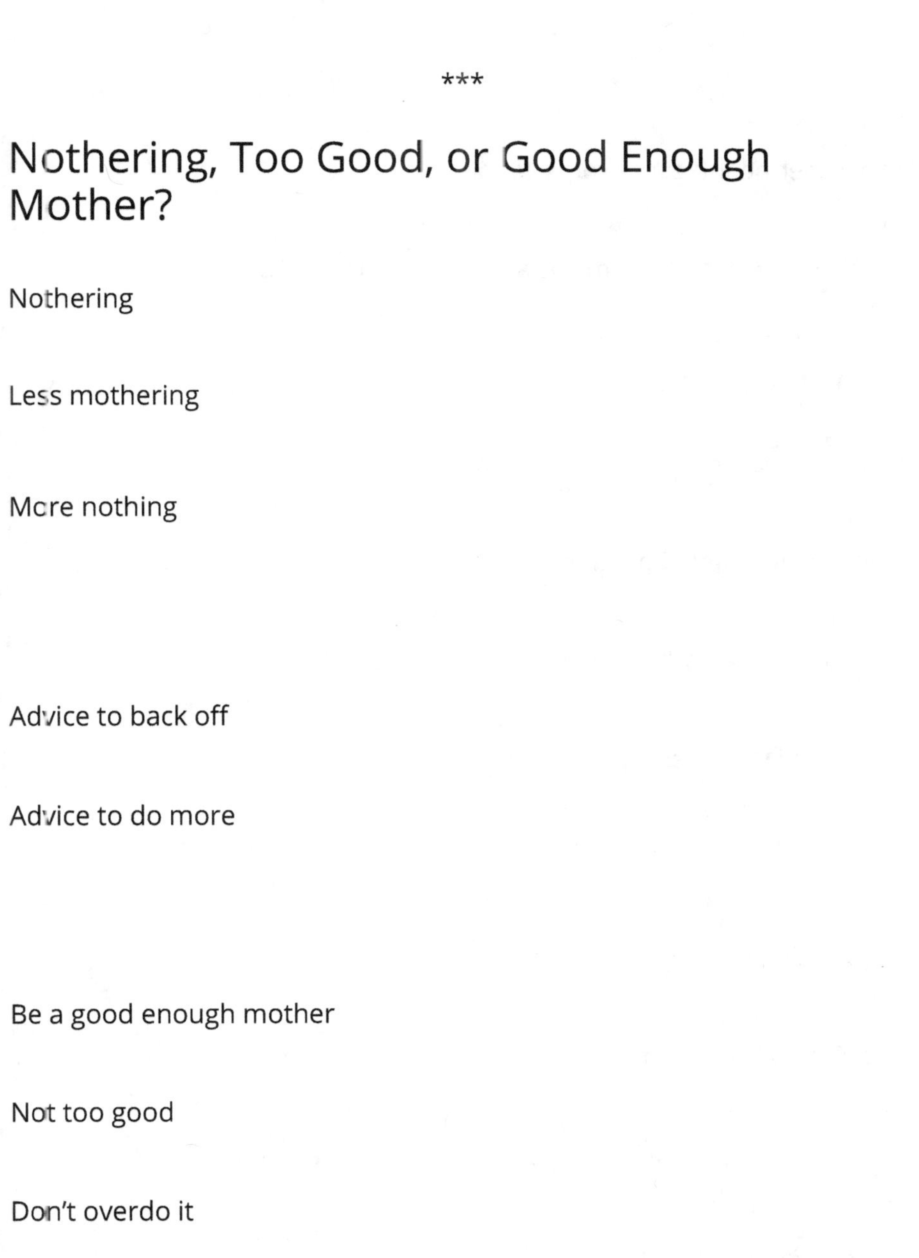

He will never be able to care for himself

He'll end up in codependent relationships

From other health care professionals

Make sure he eats three meals and three snacks a day

He doesn't eat complete meals on his own

He just eats protein bars and popcorn

Honestly, though, when I was sixteen

My lunch was a Tiger's Milk bar and Diet Coke

I am so sick of taking care of my son

My son who has had migraines and cyclic vomiting since he was a toddler

I can't even imagine living with so much pain, so much vomiting

But, I've had it with being compassionate

My patience is wearing thin

So sick of it

Fed up

Exhausted

Fuck

And, I just want to chill

To do nothing

I typed "nothering" rather than nothing

Nothering, not mothering, not nothing, but Nothering

Yes

That is what I need to do

Nothering

Less mothering

More nothing

I feel fatigue at a deep level

At a cellular level

In my bones

In the marrow of my bones

I feel tears wanting to flow

Being held back by what

By a dam

By a façade of functionality

Feminine Collective published "Good Enough Mothering," a poem of mine about mothering a migraineur, at *http://www.femininecollective.com/good-enough-mother/*

***

I'm at a Loss...

My son has missed WAY too much school this year. He's attending a private school where he gets one-on-one attention and learns at his own pace, so he simply falls behind and the charges for missed classes just keep adding up.

He had gastroenteritis earlier this year (which we all had and which we all still have lingering GI symptoms from). This morning he complained that he had a migraine. I do not know whether he truly has a migraine, for his symptoms are not as severe as they were before he took preventive medication.

Our psychiatrist has told me that I should stop taking Matthew to health care specialists, that he needs to learn to live with migraines, and that I am enabling him. Hard to have your child live with chronic, cyclic pain and vomiting. Those in the mental health profession tend to pathologize physical symptoms as "somatic" and dismiss very real suffering and pain. I, too, have been guilty of doing so in the past with both my son and my husband.

Yes, I'm at a loss as to what to do, as to how best to care for my son and myself.

***

Shedding a Few Tears

It's been a year. It's been a year since I noticed that my mother hadn't taken her turn in Words with Friends. It's been a year since my mother was verbal. It's been a year since she could use language.

Her passion was words. She spent her days playing word games. She was proud that she had been debate team captain in college. She could, and would, and did slay with words.

Last year she had a stroke. Life hasn't been the same since; not for her, not for my father, not for my sister, not for me, not for my son, not for my husband.

Finally, I allow myself to gently shed a few tears, a few soft tears. Finally, I allow myself much needed mourning the loss of my verbal mother. She is still with us, but she is different. Her brain permanently changed, permanently damaged.

I can no longer talk on the phone with her. I can no longer play word games with her. And, so, I'm sad. I miss the old her. Even if she did slay with words.

***

Mini Thanksgivings

This weekend my sister visited, and we celebrated Thanksgiving twice with our parents. Friday, we joined our mother at her memory care community and joined their festivities. That afternoon and early dinner went very well. We had fun decorating her room and organizing photos.

Saturday, we brought our father to visit our mother for lunch. The visit went well, until we left them alone for a few minutes while we got coffee in the lobby. By the time I returned to our mother's room, they were planning their escape back to their old beach house (which they no longer own. We had to sell it to pay for their care).

Big sigh. Clearly, they wish their lives were as they were before dementia, before stroke. We all do.

***

Caregiving Can Wear You Down

Since Thanksgiving weekend, I've been sick with an upper respiratory infection (URI). As an asthmatic, URIs tend to go to my lungs. My son, too, is sick and in bed (no way for a teenager to spend the weekend). URIs are highly contagious. We tend to share far too many illnesses in my family. Even our labradoodle Thumper is taking antibiotics for a cough.

Until my mother had a stroke November 2015, she was my father's caregiver. Since then, caregiving has become my responsibility, as now both my parents have dementia. My father has alcohol-related dementia (alcohol is a neurotoxin). My mother now has vascular dementia with behavioral complications (brain damage can do that) and she cannot speak.

As I live with bipolar disorder while parenting an adolescent migraineur, I couldn't care for two aging parents with dementia without help, for doing so would likely put me in a psychiatric hospital. Finding long-term care that could address their needs proved challenging. For now, we've had to separate them. Heartbreaking, but necessary for their health. To pay for their care, we had to sell their beloved beach house, for memory care is extremely expensive.

If my mother had more caregiving support before her stroke, perhaps she may not have had a stroke, perhaps she would have received more timely medical care. My mother was exhausted, stressed, and taking antidepressants (caregivers are at risk of depression). My father just thought that my mother was napping. His dementia interfered with his ability to respond to her stroke appropriately.

My mother, a caregiver, needed help, needed respite, needed care herself. My sister and I had been talking to our mother about downsizing and moving closer to my sister. But my father fought the idea of moving out of their beach house, leaving our mother essentially trapped.

Thankfully they are doing well now, given their current life circumstances. Take care of yourself. Take care of your brain. Take care of your heart. Good health is a blessing.

***

Time to Write Again?

Not Writing So Much

Taking It Easy

***

PRE-CHRISTMAS TRAVEL WRITING

I jump from one app to another. Jigsaw puzzle, to reading, to writing. Back and forth, writing and jigsaw. Uneasy. Jittery.

Uneasy. Not at ease. Tense. Guilty. Dramatic, yes, but so fucking what. That's who I am. I have no desire to change that about myself. Besides, honestly, I keep most of my drama inside.

***

BACK HOME ORGANIZING MY THOUGHTS

Haven't been writing much over this past holiday season. Left my time and energy for family and myself. Since my post-Thanksgiving chest cold, I've been doing jigsaw puzzles and not engaging in as many verbal activities.

Kind of like my mother. She nods yes, shakes her head no, or stares blankly, not seeming to understand. She no longer reads the newspaper. Just turns the pages, pulls out the ads, and organizes the paper by section. Reassuring daily routine, even if she can no longer read.

Although I visited both my parents before both Thanksgiving and Christmas, I felt guilty leaving them behind when I visited my sister and in-laws. Broke my heart. So much guilt, even though I know after trial and error, that we are giving our parents the best of care. Just can't be in two places at once.

Last year around Christmas time, my Mom was psychiatrically hospitalized. More to the point, I had her psychiatrically hospitalized. Heartbreaking decision, but I tried to do the right thing every step of the way.

We had hoped to have them living together back then. Our mother went from stroke rehab to the psychiatric hospital, then to another stroke rehab, before moving into a board and care with my father. They did not do well in the board and care, so we ended up moving them into a high-quality memory care community.

Since that time, we've found that they do better apart in separate communities. I feel terrible that I've had her in so many places, but she's stable now, and my father's health has improved. They both seem to be happy, even though they miss each other. Their memory communities arrange a weekly Skype session, so they can "see" each other.

***

VISITED MY PARENTS THIS WEEK

The new year begins. I visited my parents before and after the holidays. When visiting my mother on Sunday, I took her out shopping. We terrorized fellow shoppers as we tried to navigate using an automated cart.

Once I got back home, I debated whether I could bring her home to live with me. Our house, though, is not well suited for a stroke survivor. Bedrooms are upstairs. Our flooring is tile and hardwood. Our stairs are steep and without a landing.

Just thinking about moving my mother in, I started to ramp up, to get mildly hypomanic. I found myself unable to sleep. Instead of sleeping I researched stair treads, handrails, stair elevators, and purchasing a single-level home.

The fact remains that my own mental health is stable because I avoid stressors that trigger symptoms and cycling. I give myself time to recover. If I was a full-time caregiver of my mother, I would not be well.

Yesterday I visited my father and brought my teen son along. My son continues to miss far too much school due to illness and migraines, which frustrates me. I try. I really do. But, I can't carry a sixteen-year-old adolescent to school when he has a fever, is vomiting, or is coughing. I'm at my wit's end.

My sister and I decided to give our parents' living situation a year. They are both doing well. The quality care they receive is why.

***

Reunited and Learning ASL

My mother has moved back in with my father, back into the same memory care community (which is lovely), again sharing a room. I hope and pray it goes better this time round than last, when they isolated and refused medication and care. They love one another very much, so it is wonderful to see them together.

Missing his old home, my father asked about his old beach house, which we sold last year to pay for their care. The staff has told my dad "therapeutic white lies" about the house, such as saying that the plumbing is being repaired.

Instead of using a "therapeutic white lie," I skirted the issue, telling my dad that since my mom had her stroke, she needs care and that the house was too much work. He asked her if she wanted to live in the memory care community, she nodded her head yes (since the stroke, she hasn't been able to speak).

I told him that it was no longer her job to cook, clean, or take care of him. Up until the stroke, she was his caregiver, as he's had progressive memory loss for years. I told them that their individual needs differ now. Mom cannot use language, but dad can and should take part in community activities designed to exercise the brain and fight memory loss.

The community's social worker has started working with my mom to help her communicate her feelings. My mom didn't like using communication boards. I knew from previous attempts at using them that my mom doesn't seem to understand what the drawings on the boards represent. She didn't want to try writing either, as she knows that she simply cannot.

BUT, the social worker discovered that my mom responds to ASL (American Sign Language). So now my mom, dad, and I are using simple ASL signs to communicate. Not sure how much my father will remember due to his dementia, nor how much my mother really understands due to her stroke and vascular dementia. At least, my parents seem to enjoy learning it.

***

Who Do I Care For, Really?

Definition of caregiver: a person who provides direct care (as for children, elderly people, or the chronically ill) (Merriam-Webster)

Definition of caretaker: one that gives physical or emotional care and support (Merriam-Webster)

I spend way too much emotional and physical energy toward the care of others, aside from myself. Why do I care so much, too much? No doubt due to my upbringing, to my relationship to my parents – trying to please, to earn their love and approval. Why, after decades of therapy, do I still feel and act as an enmeshed parentified daughter? I'll just leave that question hanging there for now. Not up for explaining alcoholic family dynamics. Too tired. Adult Children of Alcoholics has a good concise description.

Who do I really care for? Good question. My husband and my son are the most important people in my life. I have devoted a great deal of time and energy trying to help my son. Too much, perhaps. No, not perhaps, without doubt. Now, I need to step back, to neglect a bit, to allow for more independence. Time to do just enough. To be just good enough. Just enough. Enough.

My sister, trying to help me set boundaries and stop taking on too much emotional responsibility, reminded me that I am not our parents' caregiver. They are in memory care. The memory care facility provides their daily care. That's what we pay them for.

I am not my parents' caregiver. I am my son's caregiver, and even he could use less of my care.

Now that my parents both have dementia and live in a memory care community, aside from being their daughter, my role is to be their power of attorney. With my sister, I make decisions on their behalf. I pay their bills. I coordinate their care, which is not the same as giving them direct care.

Before my mother's stroke, I did not visit my parents regularly. I did, though, talk and play Words with Friends with my mom daily. I miss communicating with her. I miss my parents as they were before dementia. I'm grieving.

Living with bipolar disorder, I must take care of myself. This season, spring-

time, is a time when I often start mood cycling. I feel particularly vulnerable and fatigued. The longer sunny days trigger hypomania and irritability.

On a more positive note, in January and February and again next week,
I've been a NAMI Provider Educator for the staff at the hospital where I
received both inpatient and partial day treatment twelve years ago. I enjoy
educating their staff on what it is like to live with mental illness, and to
be in mental health recovery. Wish me well next week. We're increasing
the time that we devote to our personal trauma stories, so I must rewrite
mine. I may edit my In Our Own Voice presentation for content, or I could
look at what I have shared here.

***

Sick with Dread

Frustrating to parent an adolescent who feels sick chronically. Difficult to
know if he feels sick because he is sick with a contagious disease, or if he
has a migraine, or if he is anxious. Honestly, right now, I'm feeling sick to
my stomach. Sick with dread. Dreading a summer trying to get my kid out
of his bed, out of his bedroom, out of the house, and to summer school.

***

Parenting this Kid is Isolating

This morning I attended an OC Writers' write-in. I haven't attended a writers' group in a long time. Been isolating myself and focusing on my son,
rather than my writing, rather than myself. Today, I left him home in bed,
then left the meeting early to get him to class on time. When I got back
home, he was dry-heaving in bed. Crap.

Hate spending my mornings trying to wake him up to do his homework and go to school. He will be seventeen next month. Time to wake up and do homework on his own. Unfortunately, his private school is not within walking distance, nor would it be a safe bike ride, and my kid has no interest in getting his driver's license yet. So, I'm still driving him to and from school.

The first week of June, during my son's summer break, when I didn't have to act as alarm clock and chauffeur, I started cleaning my house with help of my next-door neighbor. She did most of the cleaning and organizing. I chatted and did a wee bit of organizing. We tackled the kitchen, spending two hours on Monday and two hours on Friday.

The second week of June was my son's first week of summer school, so I took the week off cleaning and organizing. He has a full schedule this summer. He attended most of his classes last week, perhaps because I offered him $10/class/day. He's motivated by money. It costs more to reschedule his classes than it does to pay him to attend.

***

Sick of Sickness

Sick of sickness

Hitting a wall

Not moving forward

Sick of struggling

With my son's illnesses

Wish his symptoms

Both physical and mental health

Would end

Sick of my son being sick

APPENDICES

Bipolar Disorder

Bipolar disorder, also known as manic-depressive illness, is a brain disorder that causes unusual shifts in mood, energy, activity levels, and the ability to carry out day-to-day tasks.

There are four basic types of bipolar disorder; all of them involve clear changes in mood, energy, and activity levels. These moods range from periods of extremely "up," elated, and energized behavior (known as manic episodes) to very sad, "down," or hopeless periods (known as depressive episodes). Less severe manic periods are known as hypomanic episodes.

- **Bipolar I Disorder:** defined by manic episodes that last at least 7 days, or by manic symptoms that are so severe that the person needs immediate hospital care. Usually, depressive episodes occur as well, typically lasting at least 2 weeks. Episodes of depression with mixed features (having depression and manic symptoms at the same time) are also possible.

- **Bipolar II Disorder:** defined by a pattern of depressive episodes and hypomanic episodes, but not the full-blown manic episodes described above.

- **Cyclothymic Disorder (also called cyclothymia):** defined by numerous periods of hypomanic symptoms as well numerous periods of depressive symptoms lasting for at least 2 years (1 year in children and adolescents). However, the symptoms do not meet the diagnostic requirements for a hypomanic episode and a depressive episode.

- **Other Specified and Unspecified Bipolar and Related Disorders:** defined by bipolar disorder symptoms that do not match the three categories listed above.

SIGNS AND SYMPTOMS

People with bipolar disorder experience periods of unusually intense emotion, changes in sleep patterns and activity levels, and unusual behaviors. These distinct periods are called "mood episodes." Mood episodes are drastically different from the moods and behaviors that are typical for the person. Extreme changes in energy, activity, and sleep go along with mood episodes.

People having a manic episode may:

- Feel very "up," "high," or elated

- Have a lot of energy

- Have increased activity levels

- Feel "jumpy" or "wired"

- Have trouble sleeping

- Become more active than usual

- Talk really fast about a lot of different things

- Be agitated, irritable, or "touchy"

- Feel like their thoughts are going very fast

- Think they can do a lot of things at once

- Do risky things, like spend a lot of money or have reckless sex

People having a depressive episode may:

- Feel very sad, down, empty, or hopeless

- Have very little energy

- Have decreased activity levels

- Have trouble sleeping, they may sleep too little or too much

- Feel like they can't enjoy anything

- Feel worried and empty

- Have trouble concentrating

- Forget things a lot

- Eat too much or too little

- Feel tired or "slowed down"

- Think about death or suicide

Sometimes a mood episode includes symptoms of both manic and depressive symptoms. This is called an episode with mixed features. People experiencing an episode with mixed features may feel very sad, empty, or hopeless, while at the same time feeling extremely energized.

Bipolar disorder can be present even when mood swings are less extreme.

For example, some people with bipolar disorder experience hypomania, a less severe form of mania. During a hypomanic episode, an individual may feel very good, be highly productive, and function well. The person may not feel that anything is wrong, but family and friends may recognize the mood swings and/or changes in activity levels as possible bipolar disorder. Without proper treatment, people with hypomania may develop severe mania or depression.

Diagnosis

Proper diagnosis and treatment help people with bipolar disorder lead healthy and productive lives. Talking with a doctor or other licensed mental health professional is the first step for anyone who thinks he or she may have bipolar disorder. The doctor can complete a physical exam to rule out other conditions. If the problems are not caused by other illnesses, the doctor may conduct a mental health evaluation or provide a referral to a trained mental health professional, such as a psychiatrist, who is experienced in diagnosing and treating bipolar disorder.

Note for Health Care Providers: People with bipolar disorder are more likely to seek help when they are depressed than when experiencing mania or hypomania. Therefore, a careful medical history is needed to ensure that bipolar disorder is not mistakenly diagnosed as major depression. Unlike people with bipolar disorder, people who have depression only (also called unipolar depression) do not experience mania. They may, however, experience some manic symptoms at the same time, which is also known as major depressive disorder with mixed features.

Bipolar Disorder and Other Illnesses

Some bipolar disorder symptoms are similar to other illnesses, which can make it hard for a doctor to make a diagnosis. In addition, many people have bipolar disorder along with another illness such as anxiety disorder, substance abuse, or an eating disorder. People with bipolar disorder are also at higher risk for thyroid disease, migraine headaches, heart disease, diabetes, obesity, and other physical illnesses.

Psychosis: Sometimes, a person with severe episodes of mania or depression also has   psychotic symptoms, such as hallucinations or delusions. The psychotic symptoms tend to match the person's extreme mood. For example:

- Someone having psychotic symptoms during a manic episode may believe she is famous, has a lot of money, or has special powers.

- Someone having psychotic symptoms during a depressive episode may believe he is ruined and penniless, or that he has committed a crime.

As a result, people with bipolar disorder who also have psychotic symptoms are sometimes misdiagnosed with schizophrenia.

Anxiety and ADHD: Anxiety disorders and attention-deficit hyperactivity disorder (ADHD) are often diagnosed among people with bipolar disorder.

Substance Abuse: People with bipolar disorder may also misuse alcohol or drugs, have relationship problems, or perform poorly in school or at work. Family, friends and people experiencing symptoms may not recognize these problems as signs of a major mental illness such as bipolar disorder.

Risk Factors

Scientists are studying the possible causes of bipolar disorder. Most agree that there is no single cause. Instead, it is likely that many factors contribute to the illness or increase risk.

Brain Structure and Functioning: Some studies show how the brains of people with bipolar disorder may differ from the brains of healthy people or people with other mental disorders. Learning more about these differences, along with new information from genetic studies, helps scientists better understand bipolar disorder and predict which types of treatment will work most effectively.

Genetics: Some research suggests that people with certain genes are more likely to develop bipolar disorder than others. But genes are not the only risk factor for bipolar disorder. Studies of identical twins have shown that even if one twin develops bipolar disorder, the other twin does not always develop the disorder, despite the fact that identical twins share all of the same genes.

Family History: Bipolar disorder tends to run in families. Children with a parent or sibling who has bipolar disorder are much more likely to develop the illness, compared with children who do not have a family history of the disorder. However, it is important to note that most people with a family history of bipolar disorder will not develop the illness.

Treatments and Therapies

Treatment helps many people, even those with the most severe forms of bipolar disorder, gain better control of their mood swings and other bipolar symptoms. An effective treatment plan usually includes a combination of medication and psychotherapy (also called "talk therapy"). Bipolar disorder is a lifelong illness. Episodes of mania and depression typically come back over time. Between episodes, many people with bipolar disorder are free of mood changes, but some people may have lingering symptoms. Long-term, continuous treatment helps to control these symptoms.

MEDICATIONS

Different types of medications can help control symptoms of bipolar disorder. An individual may need to try several different medications before finding ones that work best.

Medications generally used to treat bipolar disorder include:

- Mood stabilizers

- Atypical antipsychotics

- Antidepressants

Anyone taking a medication should:

- Talk with a doctor or a pharmacist to understand the risks and benefits of the medication

- Report any concerns about side effects to a doctor right away. The doctor may need to change the dose or try a different medication.

- Avoid stopping a medication without talking to a doctor first. Suddenly stopping a medication may lead to "rebound" or worsening of bipolar disorder symptoms. Other uncomfortable or potentially dangerous withdrawal effects are also possible.

- Report serious side effects to the U.S. Food and Drug Administration (FDA) MedWatch Adverse Event Reporting program online at http:// www.fda.gov/Safety/MedWatch or by phone at 1-800-332-1088. Clients and doctors may send reports.

For basic information about medications, visit the NIMH Mental Health Medications `webpage`. For the most up-to-date information on medications, side effects, and warnings, visit the FDA website.

PSYCHOTHERAPY

When done in combination with medication, psychotherapy (also called "talk therapy") can be an effective treatment for bipolar disorder. It can provide support, education, and guidance to people with bipolar disorder and their families. Some psychotherapy treatments used to treat bipolar disorder include:

- Cognitive behavioral therapy (CBT)

- Family-focused therapy

- Interpersonal and social rhythm therapy

- Psychoeducation

Visit the NIMH Psychotherapies webpage to learn about the various types of psychotherapies.

OTHER TREATMENT OPTIONS

Electroconvulsive Therapy (ECT): ECT can provide relief for people with severe bipolar disorder who have not been able to recover with other treatments. Sometimes ECT is used for bipolar symptoms when other medical conditions, including pregnancy, make taking medications too risky. ECT may cause some short-term side effects, including confusion, disorientation, and memory loss. People with bipolar disorder should discuss possible benefits and risks of ECT with a qualified health professional.

Sleep Medications: People with bipolar disorder who have trouble sleeping usually find that treatment is helpful. However, if sleeplessness does not improve, a doctor may suggest a change in medications. If the problem continues, the doctor may prescribe sedatives or other sleep medications.

Supplements: Not much research has been conducted on herbal or natural supplements and how they may affect bipolar disorder.

It is important for a doctor to know about all prescription drugs, over-the-counter medications, and supplements a client is taking. Certain medications and supplements taken together may cause unwanted or dangerous effects.

Keeping a Life Chart: Even with proper treatment, mood changes can occur. Treatment is more effective when a client and doctor work closely together and talk openly about concerns and choices. Keeping a life chart that records daily mood symptoms, treatments, sleep patterns, and life events can help clients and doctors track and treat bipolar disorder most effectively.

Finding Treatment

A family doctor is a good resource and can be the first stop in searching for help.

For general information on mental health and to find local treatment services, call the Substance Abuse and Mental Health Services Administration (SAMHSA) Treatment Referral Helpline at 1-800-662-HELP (4357).

The SAMHSA website has a Behavioral Health Treatment Services Locator that can search for treatment information by address, city, or ZIP code.

Visit the NIMH's Help for Mental Illnesses webpage for more information and resources.

For Immediate Help

If You Are in Crisis: Call the toll-free National Suicide Prevention Lifeline at **1-800-273-TALK (8255)**, available 24 hours a day, 7 days a week. The service is available to anyone. All calls are confidential.

If you are thinking about harming yourself or thinking about suicide:

- Tell someone who can help right away

- Call your licensed mental health professional if you are already working with one

- Call your doctor

- Go to the nearest hospital emergency department

If a loved one is considering suicide:

- Do not leave him or her alone

- Try to get your loved one to seek immediate help from a doctor or the nearest hospital emergency room, or call 911

- Remove access to firearms or other potential tools for suicide, including medications

Join a Study

Clinical trials are research studies that look at new ways to prevent, detect, or treat diseases and conditions, including bipolar disorder. During clinical trials, treatments might be new drugs or new combinations of drugs, new surgical procedures or devices, or new ways to use existing treatments. The goal of clinical trials is to determine if a new test or treatment works and is safe. Although individual participants may benefit from being part of a clinical trial, participants should be aware that the primary purpose of a clinical trial is to gain new scientific knowledge so that others may be better helped in the future.

Please Note: Decisions about whether to apply for a clinical trial and which ones are best suited for a given individual are best made in collaboration with your licensed health professional.

How Do I Find Clinical Trials at NIMH/NIH?

Scientists at NIMH study many subjects including cognition, genetics, epidemiology, and psychiatry. The studies take place at the National Institutes of Health (NIH) Clinical Center in Bethesda, Maryland, and require regular visits. After the initial phone interview, participants come to an appointment at the clinic and meet with a clinician. Visit Join a Study: Bipolar Disorder – Adults or Join a Study: Bipolar Disorder – Children for more information.

How Do I Find a Clinical Trial Near Me?

To find a clinical trial anywhere in the world, visit ClinicalTrials.gov. This is a searchable database of federally and privately supported clinical trials conducted in the United States and around the globe. ClinicalTrials.gov has information about a trial's purpose, who may participate, locations, and phone numbers for more details. Anyone interested in joining a clinical trial should consult a health professional before making a commitment.

Source: National Institute of Mental Health (2016). Bipolar Disorder. Retrieved March 18, 2018 from https://www.nimh.nih.gov/health/topics/bipolar-disorder/index.shtml.

Mental Health Resources

Crisis Lines

- National Suicide Prevention Lifeline

    - suicidepreventionlifeline.org

    - 1-800-273-TALK (8255)

- Veterans Crisis Line: 1-800-273-8255 press 1

Find Treatment

- MentalHealth.gov
- Substance Abuse and Mental Health Services Administration

    - findtreatment.samhsa.gov

Support & Information

- Depression and Bipolar Support Alliance: DBSAlliance.org

- National Alliance on Mental Illness: NAMI.org

- International Bipolar Foundation: IBPF.org

Research

- Brain & Behavior Research Foundation: bbrfoundation.org

- National Institute of Mental Health: NIMH.NIH.gov